BOOKWORM

A Memoir of Childhood Reading

By the same author

A Twisted Root
Asking for Trouble

Brian Moore: a Biography
Elizabeth Bowen

As editor:

The Ulster Anthology
The Oxford Book of Detective Stories
The Belfast Anthology
The Oxford Book of Ireland
Twelve Irish Ghost Stories
The Oxford Book of Travel Stories
The Oxford Book of Schooldays
The Oxford Book of Modern Women's Stories
Julia Symons at 80: A Tribute
The Rattle of the North
The Penguin Book of British Comic Writing
The Penguin Book of Brititsh Comic Stories
The Oxford Book of English Detective Stories

With Mary Cadogan:

The Lady Investigates
Women and Children First
You're a Brick, Angela!

BOOKWORM

A Memoir of Childhood Reading

Patricia Craig

SOMERVILLE PRESS

Somerville Press Ltd,
Dromore, Bantry,
Co. Cork, Ireland

First published 2015

Designed by Jane Stark
Typeset in Adobe Caslon Pro
seamistgraphics@gmail.com

ISBN: 978-0-9927364-5-3

Printed and bound in Spain
by GraphyCems, Villatuerta, Navarra

LOTTERY FUNDED

For Fiona (Devlin) Coyle
and Mary (Stinson) Cosgrove
old school friends

And in memory of Mary Cadogan

There are no days more full in childhood than those days that are not lived at all, the days lost in a book.

John McGahern, *Memoir*

CONTENTS

Chalet des Courlis
Wimereux-sur-Mer.

Rose Lawn
Kingsgate
Broadstairs,
Kent.

July 24th, 1953

Dear Patricia Craig,

Thank you very much, my dear, for your very
nice letter. I am glad that you like the Bunter
books, and certainly I intend to write a great many
more, as well as Tom Merry's annual and Billy
Bunter's annual for a long time to come. I am
sorry that I have no old Magnets or Gems or
Populars or Holiday Annuals. I gave my collection
to the Salvage in the War time, and have never
been able to replace it.   But I have found an old
"Schoolboys' Own" book, in which two or three old
Magnets are reprinted in a single long story, and
I am sending you this, and hope that you may like
it. The story in it came out in two or three
numbers of the Magnet: so, you see, it is just the
same as a Magnet.

With kindest regards,
Very sincerely,

Frank Richards

Letter from Frank Richards to the young Patricia Craig: see p. 116

PREFACE

Aren't you coming out, Mary?
Come out – your eyes will tire.
Oh let me be, please, please, said she,
I want to read by the fire.
Eleanor Farjeon, 'Mary Indoors'

THIS IS A BOOK ABOUT READING, about the ways in which an addiction set going in childhood will persist throughout one's life. It's obvious that, as one grows older, one's tastes in literature will expand and deepen; but my specific concern here – children's books – cuts out any serious consideration of key works encountered in later life. Instead, I am setting out to revisit my former existence as a post-war, Northern Irish, juvenile, alacritous picker-up of every variety of enchantment to be found between the covers of a book. The project includes elements of autobiography, topography, literary criticism, local history (Belfast) – in however limited or subjective a form. It's a personal account of a kind of imaginative euphoria, based on reading. Reading to foster *joie de vivre*, to banish tedium, to instill a sense of life's resources. A capacity for total immersion – which is what I possessed – is essential to the process. I and other childhood story devotees embarked, at the earliest possible moment, on an endless succession of book-adventures to boost our store of exhilaration and add a decorative layer to our workaday experiences. We were set apart from the half-hearted reading brigade among our contemporaries, those whose enjoyment of a story was only minimal. They could take it or leave it; for us it was a matter of necessity. Whatever fell within our reading grasp, we lapped it up.

Of course, personal preference came into the business early on. We exercised a kind of critical discrimination, albeit a frivolous kind. Some stories recommended by our elders, or others mistakenly selected from a library shelf, proved uncongenial. For myself, any book I judged didactic or old-fashioned was guaranteed to get up my would-be avant-garde nose, and anything containing an overt moral ruled itself out by definition. A *covert* moral, on the other hand, was perfectly acceptable, tied up as it was with the highest form of social adjustment, and denoting nothing more than an attractive (fictional) personality.

At no time during my life have I altogether relinquished an affectionate attitude towards children's books. As I say in Chapter Two, a break occurred in my reading of juvenile literature roughly between the ages of fourteen or fifteen and twenty-five: the years during which I was most anxious to appear properly grown-up. Whenever I needed to replenish my stock of reading material, it was the adult, not the children's, section of the nearest public library I gravitated towards. But even at this time, lapses into juvenility on my part weren't unknown. I seem to remember that it was Enid Blyton's 'St Clare's' and 'Malory Towers' series that saw me through a bout of flu as I coughed and sniffed in an attic room of a Victorian house in West Hampstead, London, in 1965 or thereabouts. (I was then a student at the Central School of Art.)

Mention of those Blyton titles brings me to the (inevitable) subject of rereading. Obviously, any consideration of one-time literary pursuits will entail a new approach to previously cherished material. You have to hold a lot of things in mind – the original delight, the sober-sided reappraisal, the various atmospheres pertaining to past allurement and present reclamation. An insightful, entertaining and clear-headed study by the American academic and critic Patricia Meyer Spacks, *On Rereading* (2011), which recently came my way, illumines the entire procedure. Unlike this author's, though, my purpose is not to examine in detail the discrepancy between first and subsequent readings, to see what strikes one the second, or twenty-second, time around. (Propelled by the story's momentum, you might, on a first encounter, have skimmed over glaring holes – or, on the other hand, in your haste to reach the denouement, have failed to register narrative strategies and implications.) It's more that I want to create a web of recollections, observations and associations, with a good selection of children's books at its centre.

And there is another aspect of book fixation to consider. I write not only as a reader and rereader, but also as a collector, a besotted pursuer of first editions and dust-jackets: a personal idiosyncrasy added on top of the reading habit, which has filled my life (and my bookshelves) with hundreds of highly charged, colourful and delectable volumes (or pieces of moonshine). It is these I have fallen upon, over and over, while charting the progress of a bookworm.

Patricia Craig
Antrim
June 2014

1. JIM, JOCK and JUMBO

The overlapping and haunting of life by fiction began ... before there was anything to be got from the printed page; it began from the day one was old enough to be told a story or shown a picture book.

Elizabeth Bowen, 'Out of a Book', *Orion 111* (1946)

MY EARLIEST EXPOSURE TO THE printed word was not auspicious. Before I could read, I could wield a destructive pencil – and no one thought to intervene as I sat on the hearth rug with my coloured crayons, merrily disfiguring page after page. Anything to keep me amused. The pages, fortunately, were mostly in old school exercise books; but other pages, printed pages, received the same disgraceful treatment. Some were so horribly damaged that they had to be thrown away. A couple of Greyfriars Holiday Annuals belonging to my mother and a lot of school readers suffered mutilation at my hands. Later, I'd be appalled at the depredations carried out by my uncomprehending self – a vandal in a floppy sun bonnet and pink rosebud dress with a smocked yoke. Or, according to the season, in a minuscule knitted jumper over a Liberty bodice and woollen knickers.

Time was passing. My mother, whose absence had probably contributed to my blitz on books, was back at home following her wartime job in the Censorship Office at Stormont, where she spent her days at a desk scrutinising letters from the troops and erasing anything remotely detrimental to national security. You could say that my occupation was a parody of hers. German spies in Friardale – out! Loder's uncle dropped behind enemy lines – scratch, scribble! But now the war had ended, leaving behind its residue of air-raid shelters and ration books. My grandmother stood in the scullery in a flowered overall making soda bread, or preparing some other indigenous dish such as scallion champ. For a special occasion there was apple potato bread cooked on the griddle, swimming in butter and brown sugar. Yum. My mother baked buns and, on rainy afternoons, made pan toffee to cheer things up. Not that rain was a trial to me: on the contrary, I relished it, even when it dripped off the corrugated iron roof of the coal-hole in our back yard, or saturated the old pine table kept out there as a repository for odds and ends, including a sad stuffed squirrel and a green-and-gold, urn-shaped, broken vase. Damp and coal dust still disseminate a whiff of the charmed life, as far as I am concerned.

The kitchen in our house, hardly bigger than a cupboard, was called the scullery, while the living-room, which was also the dining-room, was known as the kitchen. (The front room, called the sitting-room, was only pressed into service at Christmas, when a fire was lit in its otherwise unused grate, and a wonderful, unique atmosphere pervaded it.) A large sash window, set quite high up in the kitchen wall, looked out over our back garden and along St James's Avenue with its row of plane trees, and the lamp post commandeered for swinging by neighbourhood children. To obtain a view from this window, I had to scramble on to the back of the sofa which sat below it, clutching the flimsy cotton curtains to pull myself up. With the exception of a few weeks in summer, a coal fire was started in the kitchen first thing every morning, and kept going all day to heat the boiler and provide hot water. A wire-mesh guard stood in front of the fire to keep sparks from landing on the green-and-brown, art deco hearth rug – or on the infant despoiler sitting on it.

The coal, which arrived once a week on a horse-drawn cart, was deposited in the yard by a dusty-faced coalman who carried it in, bent double, in a sack on his back. I called him Mr Grimes, after Tom's persecutor in *The Water Babies*, though I understood he wasn't actually a chimney-sweep. The sweep was a different person, whose generic habitation was a crooked little house at the corner of Bradbury Place, a tram-ride away from us. It was quaintly dubbed 'the wee sweep's house'. But 'Grimes' seemed right for someone saturated in coal dust. Books, story books, were beginning to supply points of reference, as I grasped the connection between stories that were told to me, and the objects I had appropriated for scribbling-pads. Nothing would do me now but to learn to read. Because I had lots of nursery rhymes by heart, and could recite these with the book open in front of me at the relevant page, people thought I *was* reading; and neighbours were invited in to marvel at the precocious child – which can't have done much to burnish my character, or enhance my subsequent standing among my peers (those who were reminded of this supposed proficiency). Fortunately I developed a hefty dose of shyness to counteract the smarty-pants syndrome (one just about as appealing as the other) – and indeed, I would like to think that both these character defects began to vanish with the actual acquisition of reading ability. Exactly when it was that the marks on the page fell into place to form intelligible words, I cannot remember. But from that moment on, I became one of those children of whom it is said, either indulgently or disparagingly, that their nose is always stuck in a book.

There weren't too many of us at the Falls Road end of the Donegall Road, or in St James's Avenue, but we reading children sought one another out, to compare notes, to receive recommendations, to borrow whatever was available for borrowing, to discuss authors and plots to our hearts' content. What delighted us most was subjecting ourselves to the enhancing power of fiction. But this, the sociable aspect of reading, can't have occurred before I was six or seven, at least, and after public lending libraries had entered into the picture. Where did the books come from, in the early pre-library days? Well, our house had more than most, some kept high up in a corner cupboard out of the reach of marauding infant hands. Nursery rhymes, of course; Grimm's Fairy Tales, *The Water Babies*, *Wuthering Heights*, my mother's text books from Queen's University, Palgrave's *Golden Treasury*, the Lyrical Ballads of Wordsworth and Coleridge, and so on. Not all of these were readable by me, indeed, at this stage; but it pleased me to know they were there. I admired the stubbornness of Wordsworth's little cottage girl who refuses to accord defunct status to two of her brothers and sisters, even though their names are clearly marked on gravestones in the cemetery. 'We Are Seven.' I wasn't really sure what it meant, being dead; but I was sure it was something that would never happen to me, or to anyone I cared about, down to the dog Kim. It had happened to another Wordsworth character, Lucy Gray: but poor Lucy has an incredibly thoughtless father who sends her out into an oncoming blizzard to guide her mother home from a nearby town, when he must be aware there are dangers out on the moor for a child blinded by snow. Why couldn't he have gone himself? Her mother gets home perfectly well under her own steam anyway; it's Lucy who is lost. I thought this was a sensible way to read the poem, or at least to interpret its argument, when it was read to me; probably I would still have had difficulty with words like 'solitary' and 'minster-clock'.

Once I can read with no bother, there's a brief period – some months? a year? – when a book comes into the house each Friday, bought by my youthful father out of his weekly wage packet from the Ulster Transport Authority at Duncrue

Street where he works as a mechanic fitting together parts of trains. By this means, a good selection of volumes in the 'Blackie's Easy to Read' series comes into my possession. Curious Kate, the calf with a predilection for jamming her head in a hen-coop – where are you now? What's become of *Dame Trot and her Cat*, with the picturesque cover by Rosa Petherick? Who now cherishes *The Magic Duck*? These I loved for a time, but, once outgrown, bit by bit they found their way to an annual school jumble sale, or Fancy Fair, along with *The Splendid Book for Tinies* and an abridged *Tom Sawyer*.

Other books arrived from different sources. A scruffy *Mickey Mouse Annual* had come via an older cousin, I think; it sat on a shelf in the kitchen/living room next to the bakelite wireless, and wasn't much to my taste. It pandered to the worst kind of juvenile rumbustiousness, I thought with six-year-old severity, and the reading material it offered was simply silly. Who wanted to read, 'Away they went with a BANG and a POP and a ROAR!'? Not me: I had better means of getting transported to a magical realm. I had *Brogeen of the Stepping-Stones*, with its country fairs and whistling tinkers and its agitated leprechaun; and, above all, I had *The Enchanted Wood* with the Dorothy Wheeler dust-jacket awash in woodland whimsy, and the 'dreadfully queer' lands, one after another, located at the top of an unusual tree, accessible only to lucky children named Jo, Bessie and Fanny, but enabling the rest of us, vicariously, to walk on air.

Mickey Mouse held none of this magic. However, on the

credit side, its cover radiated a seasonal cheeriness, with the mice and Goofy engaging in a bit of carol singing beneath the window of an infuriated duck in a nightcap. I liked things to be suitably seasonal. A different carol-singing scene, though, this time on the cover of a Daily Express *Rupert Annual*, was more to my liking. It featured the Nutwood Bear in his red winter coat holding a lantern in the snow, with his animal friends gathered round him projecting a Christmas cosiness to the fullest degree.

An aunt in England had sent that *Rupert*; other relatives, closer to home, kept up a supply of *Daily Mail Annuals* over a four- or five-year period. I must have been older then, for I was conscious of the short story's lesser power to absorb the attention. However, the miscellany of stories, puzzles, articles and illustrations had its own appeal. The *Daily Mails* had predecessors. Annuals and picture books loomed large in the beginning, stacked on those wartime bookshelves of our house on the Donegall Road. As I remember it, the jolly Bruin Boys (heroes of the *Rainbow*), all stripes and smiles, get themselves into one inflated pickle after another, raising a smile (I imagine) on my three-year-old mug; while a chubby trio known as Peter, Pauline and Fluff (the last a pup), for ever initiate some nursery jape, also to my mild amusement. I am easily amused. But not as easily as certain immature contemporaries, comic-addicts, who revel in the *Beano* and the *Dandy*, and the wham-bang antics therein. Slapstick was never my solace. I preferred the sedateness of

Rupert to the rowdiness of Biffo the Bear. I looked for the rudiments of a story, at least, not just incessant commotion. The Rupert mix – an idealised suburban decorum with magical activity added – fulfilled nearly all of a five-year-old's literary needs. Rupert by this time (the late 1940s) had acquired his strongest image at the hands of Alfred Bestall, who injected a degree of liveliness into Mary Tourtel's inspired but homely creation. The Tourtel Rupert lived in a wood before being relocated, courtesy of Bestall, to an archetypal English village with its scope for holiday fun and games (Rupert never seems to have to go to school); and the little bear's earliest adventures, for all their charm, smacked a bit too fearfully of fee-fi-fo-fum. Bestall's Rupert keeps a necessary quaintness, but he's a degree or two less quaint, and his doings are presented with a bit more gusto. He's for ever depicted whizzing through the air on a colourful mission, or seeking some other form of magical help to alleviate an injustice. ('He says, my castle's on the hill/But for those thieves I'd live there still.') And all this without a flicker of trepidation passing over his anthropomorphised face. Rupert in this respect differs from all the beaming and boisterous giraffes and tigers of Mrs Bruin's academy, and from similar alliterative animal tearaways like Bobby Bear and Teddy Tail. His facial expression is subject to very little variation, and this confers on him a certain aplomb. He takes it all in his stride, ferocious canine woodsmen and dark dungeons and woolly-haired cannibal chiefs in search of their supper. But of course the little boy/bear is never too far away from the enfolding comfort and charmed propriety of Nutwood, with its antique accoutrements – the cottagey houses and hollyhock gardens, the village green, the old-fashioned parents in their turn-of-the-century clothes. And for us too, his readers, the sense of safety and cosiness spills over into our everyday surroundings, making the fire burn with that much brighter a glow, and local landmarks assume a more compelling presence.

Our neighbourhood can do with a bit of enhancement, that's for sure. It's an assortment of two-storey, red-brick houses, some semi-detached like ours, and some standing back from the pavement in short unremarkable rows. Our house is on the corner of St James's Avenue and the Donegall Road, and boasts two bay windows, an upper and a lower. A privet hedge separates us from our elderly neighbours, Mr and Mrs Clarke. A short paved path leads from the front door with its stained-glass panel to a wooden gate, and the hedge continues round the corner into the avenue. My father is often out at weekends with his hedge-clippers restricting its growth. In the meagre front garden is the stump of a tree, long since felled. Another tree, a sally tree, I think, grows at the side of the house and fails to disclose an entrance to a fantastic land, however high up it I climb. But long before I've reached climbing age, I sit contentedly in a swing suspended from an arched gateway in a trellis arrangement which separates the tree, and the back garden, from the front. The trellis is rather wonky and rotten, and will soon be taken down. The swing has wooden bars to keep me from falling out, and a watchful adult nearby has the task of administering a push.

The front gate opens on to the Donegall Road with its whirr of trams (soon to be replaced by buses) and its side streets opposite leading to the Bog Meadows, where vegetable allotments, which flourished during the war, are still a good source of peas and beans in season. The Plots – in local parlance, the Plats: a designation that puzzles me, since I can't for the life of me see a connection between vegetables for our dinner, and a way of doing one's hair.

A left-hand turn at the gate points you towards Celtic Park, a vast greyhound-racing stadium surrounded by corrugated iron fencing, and, on the other side of the road, a couple of factories, Maguire & Patterson's match factory and one other, I think, and running between them a street called Rodney Parade, about which the inhabitants of our part of the road take a rather snooty attitude. Rodney Parade is an inferior place to live, being close to the Bog Meadows proper where tinkers park their gaudy caravans, and small grubby boys in short trousers go with their jam-jars in pursuit of spricklies. Once past the Bog Meadows, going down the Donegall Road, you are into Protestant territory and immediately cut off from any prospect of social interaction. You sit tight on the bus until it brings you to interdenominational Shaftesbury Square and Great Victoria Street, where the ambience is neutral. It's not that you feel the smallest unease, passing from one sectarian quarter to another, just that a faint sense of irreversible incompatibility is tied into the streets and shops beyond the Clowney River and the Donegall Road end of Broadway. The people who live and work there have nothing to do with you.

It's a time of skipping ropes, corner shops and Saturday afternoon matinées at the Broadway Cinema on the Falls Road. Turning right at our front gate takes you up to the intersection of the Donegall Road with the Falls, a hundred yards away, where people, shops, traffic and goings-on engender a local hubbub. At the top of the road on one corner stands Caffola's Ice-Cream Parlour, where I am sent at a later date for pokes and sliders topped with raspberry sauce; and on the other corner, McGinleys' the grocers. Dan McGinley is the owner of our house, the person to whom rent is paid by the week. He and his brother Joe run the shop, and a more unalike pair of brothers it is hard to imagine. One, the married one, is small, dark and bustling; the other, the bachelor, large, sandy and gruff. They'd make a fitting cartoon duo, going through some slapstick routine instead of spending their days slicing bacon and weighing bags of tea. The shop itself, with its high wooden counter and shelves crammed with regular 1940s' groceries, resembles the kind of place to which Rupert Bear might be sent on an errand (the prelude to an adventure). During my earliest days, with my hit-or-miss grasp of reality, Dan McGinley is associated in my mind with the character in the song about the stone outside Dan Murphy's door, and the stone itself has a precise location up the Whiterock Road.

I can't sing, and never will be able to sing, but I have by heart the words of many songs and poems (not just nursery rhymes). I enjoy having narrative verses recited to me: 'Young Lochinvar', for example, coming at top speed out of the west to disrupt a wedding party and make off with the bride. And another daredevil gallop, this time taking place during the American War of Independence and featuring a girl called Jenny McNeill, is a particular pleasure. Its opening verse, by posing the rhetorical question, 'But why should men do all the deeds/On which the love of a patriot feeds?' is possibly responsible for inclining me towards a feminist position in later life (why indeed?). But at the time, it's the exhilaration of the chase, with the rock-strewn hillside, the lashing rain and the bullets whizzing past the heroine's unruffled head, which engages my attention, along with the high drama of the style: '... Into the night the gray horse strode,/His shoes struck fire from the rocky road ...'. It is thrilling to contemplate the bravery of this eighteenth-century American teenager, and the happy outcome of her venture. (We're aware that she is fifteen, because the poem tells us so. This is an unimaginable age to me then.)

What else? 'Little Red Riding Hood' with its Northern Forest pungency and *frisson* of menace, the girl in her red cloak setting out gaily with her basket of goodies, unaware, until the final confrontation, of what is waiting to pounce on her at her grandmother's cottage. 'All the better to EAT you.' Squirm, happy horror: we know it isn't real, though it taps into all kinds of aboriginal fears. Of course, in some versions, the tale reaches a satisfactory conclusion; but it's years and years before the buoyant Angela Carter comes along to apply her subversive skills to the traditional story. *Her* Red Riding Hood can afford to laugh in his face, when the wolf bares his teeth: 'She knew she was nobody's meat.' This is a merry outcome: we might wish for a comparable defiance to be visited on the Little Match Girl, but her author has designs on our heart-strings, not our spirits; she's formed to induce in readers a sense of pathos, a poor child for ever excluded from the warmth of happy families, viyella pyjamas and cocoa at bedtime in a mug adorned with Felix-the-Cat. This Hans Andersen character is one of the archetypes geared to foster in juvenile readers an impulse of compassion, a proper, if as yet rudimentary, response to the afflictions of others. It's not at all the same thing as sentimentality, which comes at you in great sickly globs like piped synthetic cream rosettes. The execrable Pollyanna, for example, has the latter in lorryloads; while the heroes and heroines of the folk- or fairy tale are effective representations of fundamental ideas and conditions, and repositories of infinitely complex reverberations to boot.

I loved 'The Snow Queen' in particular, with the roof-apartments, gables and leaning chimneys of old Copenhagen, the reindeer, the splinter of glass entering malleable Kay's heart, and steadfast Gerda standing in her short-sleeved dress with the snow whirling round her (according to the illustration in the old school lesson book appropriated by me). This one, too, has the doughty Robber Girl whose ambiguities I enjoy: 'Not quite bad and not quite good', as another of my mother's alluring recitations, Charlotte Mew's 'The Changeling', puts it, in a different context. The wild wet wood: now there's an atmosphere to steep yourself in.

One oddity in our house is a picture book called *Jim, Jock and Jumbo*. It is published by the American firm of Dutton, and how it found its way to the Donegall Road in downbeat Belfast I have no idea. But there it was – and here it still is, in front of me, its lithographed pages as crisp and colourful as they were in 1946, when the image of a mother snail wheeling its offspring in a minuscule pram, while a traffic policeman sees them safely across the road, would have tickled my infant fancy. That the policeman is a blue velvet elephant with pink ears merely ratchets up the entertainment value a notch or two. This book has escaped the terrible incontinent crayoning that went on at the time; perhaps it was only those that made no sense to me which got themselves lined up for defacement. A lion, a hippopotamus and a sky-blue elephant living together in the jungle, on the other hand, made perfect sense, and if the hippopotamus went down with toothache at one point – well, its teeth were big enough to make that not a trifling complaint. The author of this striking work, I now discover, was Lars Borman, though much of its impact was due to Einar Norelius who drew the pictures. These names were so foreign that they would have affected me not a whit, if I ever noticed them. I was far from the stage of assessing and grading authors according to an agenda of my own. (Once I'd reached that stage, one name – that of Enid Blyton – went to the top of the list and stuck there for some time.) Indeed, I was hardly aware of stories as having an origin in the mind of an author; they just seemed an indispensable feature of the world around me, as much a part of everyday life as the clouds in the sky, or the red-brick houses of St James's Avenue.

If I close my eyes and conjure up St James's Avenue, I see its pavements and plane trees, the thick hedge enclosing our back garden, Murphy's next door and then McGrogan's. It is a short avenue, four houses on one side and seven on the other side, our side. Among the latter are two located enticingly at the end of a long paved pathway, which places this semi-detached pair at the centre of a rectangle encompassing the Avenue, the Donegall Road, the Falls Road and St James's Park. Back gardens, hedges and fences surround them. At an angle to these half-hidden houses off the Avenue is another, similar pair, whose approach is from St James's Park. I'd have been overjoyed to live in any one of them, purely on account of their unusual setting, which to my mind seemed to place them at a slight remove from reality – was that Rupert Bear I spied, lighting an autumn bonfire in one of their gardens?

But our house was perfectly all right, with its yard and shed, its lilac tree and gooseberry bush and slatted wooden seat reposing in the garden.

As the 1940s draws to a close, I am getting to grips with different quarters of my city, Belfast, and subconsciously registering the change of atmosphere between one district and the next. It's a far cry, for example, from the smoky, cobble-stoned, workaday dilapidation of the Lower Falls, to the lawns and shrubs of sedate Malone, where my new school is situated. Or from the great-department-store buzz of the city centre, to the unkempt fields and streams and hedgerows straggling upwards beyond the cemetery and a recent housing estate, towards our local landmark the Black Mountain, with its famous field in the shape of a hatchet. It all adds, *pace* Louis MacNeice, to the intoxication of things being various.

Seasonal differentiations, as I've indicated, are important too.

> January brings the snow,
> Makes our feet and fingers glow.

It does, it does, and no one under the age of ten abhors the discomforts of sopping wet woollen gloves or frozen feet. The first flurry of properly wintry weather ushers in an outbreak of snowballing and makeshift sleds for tobogganing in La Salle Drive. When a bleach-pale sun comes out, it adds an element of exhilaration. Deep and crisp and even. But it's best of all when snow comes down in thick cotton-wool blobs, swirling and swirling with hypnotic effect, so you can't quite tell if you're in our own bedroom looking out, or have got, like Alice, into a realm of intriguing derangement. First snow, says J.B. Priestley, 'is a magical event'. You go to bed in one kind of world and wake up to find yourself in another – and if that's not enchantment, he doesn't know what is. Quite so.

Snow is one thing, and the weather for going about clad in a seersucker sundress, another.

> Hot July brings cooling showers,
> Apricots, and gillyflowers.

And every real-life, voluptuous exposure to heat or hurricane, frost or wind, has its corresponding book-embodiment. 'After an hour of pedalling in the hot sun they reached the ruined castle. ... "Oh, it's lovely here!" Barbara cried, in sheer delight' (in *Rungate Manor* by Arthur Waterhouse). Sheer delight it is. I might have read this item of sub-Blyton banality in 1950 or thereabouts, without critical dissent. The ruined castle is an especially alluring motif, however superficially it's framed. And my part of the world is actually quite abundant in tumbledown castles, once you get beyond the city proper. 'Ardglass; or, The Ruined Castles' is the title of an eighteenth-century poem by the Reverend Samuel Burdy, which won't come to my attention for a good many years; but the ruins it denotes are there from the start, to be visited on day excursions by train or bus, and admired for their venerability. Closer to home – and mentioned by Cathal O'Byrne in his book *As I Roved Out* – are the remnants of Castle Robin on Colin Mountain: 'a lock of oul' stones', as the decomposed stronghold is described to O'Byrne by a local woman when he goes to take a look at it (c. 1946). Other castles I know are in a state of remarkable preservation, like Carrickfergus, or redolent of an absolute romantic cliff-edge decay, like spectacular Dunluce on the north Antrim coast. Some, like Monea Castle in County Fermanagh, are outside my range of access and familiar only from drawings or photographs. But all their 'time-worn stones', like those of what an old lesson book in my possession calls 'the grim old Tower of London', set off amorphous historical images and associations in any susceptible head.

Numerous authors have borrowed the castle ambience to ginger up a pedestrian plot, and I'll take a look at a couple of these in Chapter Two. The ruined castle is a summer emblem, by and large, a place of holiday activity. But for the moment I'm still at 551 Donegall Road, Belfast, reading *Rainy Day Stories* by Enid Blyton, perhaps ('It poured with rain that evening and the teddy bear got drenched through'), as a complement to the actual rain coming down in buckets, drumming its heels like a child in a tantrum on the coal-hole's corrugated roof, and turning the gardens and hedges and pavements of St James's Avenue to a sodden arrangement of intensified greys and greens. ... Or, if I'm ten or eleven, say, it might be *Crusoe Island* my nose is embedded in, with the enterprising Lockett children caught in a storm before finding themselves marooned in a cottage with flood waters rising about their ears. Right at the start of this wet-weather imbroglio, 'Here's the rain,' announces matter-of-fact Bill. And here it is.

> Anyone riding through it without a mackintosh would be soaked to the skin within five minutes. Indeed so violent was this first torrential onslaught that it is doubtful whether one could have seen clearly enough to battle forward along the road upon which the rain lashed down in such abandoned fury.
>
> The children crouched under the hedge, pressed tightly against one another. Above them the heavens opened – a great reservoir with the bottom fallen out. The thunder roared and crashed. The lightning zigzagged in terrifying fashion.

Thank you, M.E.Atkinson, for an absolute immersion in a waterlogged situation and compelling narrative to boot. And thank you, Harold Jones, for depicting the exigency so evocatively. Pictures and conversations, as required by Alice in her reading matter, embellish this agreeable children's novel. But I'm getting ahead of myself here (again). Say I'm still six or so, and somehow I have got my hands on a *Blackie's Children's Annual* from 1914. (The pre-Christmas St Dominic's Fancy Fair in the basement of the school on the Falls Road is a good source of second-hand books.) This annual, among other things, contains a charming illustration in colour by Florence Harrison showing a pair of girls in hooded rain capes splish-splashing along a cobbled street complete with fairy-tale houses and people carrying umbrellas in the background. 'Then Poll and I, we just pretend/We're crossing the Atlantic,' goes the caption. The accompanying verse, a long way after Robert Louis Stevenson, is not very demanding. But the picture says something essential to me about my eccentric liking for rainy weather.

Weather and seasons make an obvious way of getting in touch with the pungency of the world (the world in its pared-down, Belfast incarnation, that is. I don't know any other). There's a reason why every Christmas story features lashings of snow, and why book-days at the seaside are invariably sunny (though in real life, the bleak beaches of Portstewart or Ballyholme possess a deep attraction too). Some nearly generic titles – *At Seaside Cottage*, *Spring Comes to Nettleford*, *Snow Before Christmas* – announce an atmosphere before you even get down to reading the first page, as well as offering an unspoken guarantee of seasonal suitability, to chime with an evolving sense of how things ought to be. (A mild December is simply *wrong*, when you're six or seven.) Immemorial rituals and regulations help to impose a shape on fly-away time (or so it seems in retrospect). Though we, my contemporaries and I, are not in the least aware of it, we are measuring out our lives with rubber balls and bats, roller skates, buckets-and-spades, blackberrying cans, indoor games, Christmas cribs.

And it was always thus. This is how the poet John Hewitt encapsulates time and seasons when he looks back on his orderly Edwardian childhood in north Belfast:

Strung chestnuts every autumn; kites in spring;
girls skipping; slides and snowballs in the snow;
all those activities which bore the names
of May-Queen, Kick-the-Tin, and Rally-o.

He also, in 'The Romantic', mocks his tendency to magnify events in his highly active imagination:

When the first white flakes
fall out of the black Antrim sky
I toboggan across Alaska.

Crossing the Atlantic, tobogganing across Alaska: it's all part of the lifelong quest for headiness and significance. Life starts getting irradiated by literature (literature in the broadest sense) early on. Well, this is true for some of us at any rate: we who make up a confederacy of under-age bibliophiles. And for us, once we've attained the age of reason, the public lending library is the breath of life.

I shall get to some mid-twentieth-century libraries of Belfast in a minute, but in the meantime (bear with me) I am still projecting myself backwards into an extremely circumscribed environment. First comes the house, plain Belfast red brick, with its yard and shed and small back garden; and beyond it pavements and plane trees, and dark green ribbed metal lamp posts which call to mind Robert

Louis Stevenson's Leerie. ('With lantern and with ladder he comes posting up the street.') The associations of infancy strike deep, however overlaid they become with pseudo-recollections and impressions. There's a place (in my head) in which I'm being for ever conducted by neighbourhood big girls (nine or ten years old) along the pathways or grassy stretches of the enticing, fraught-with-perils Falls Park (you might tumble into the brown gurgling stream at one end of it and turn into an indigenous Water Baby – or get your shoes and socks covered in mud and risk chastisement at home). Or the same girls might have seated me in a swing in the drear playground beyond the grassless waste stretch by the Globe Laundry, and stood by to catch me if I should fall. Sensations and improvisations: close your eyes, think of the past, and all manner of ramifying reverberations will enter in, half-willed, half arriving willy nilly out of the blue. You didn't know your subconscious harboured so much hustle-and-bustle! And much of it gone, evaporated like a dream, before another waft of recollection takes its place.

All heartfelt but airy-fairy. To return to brass tacks: it's a day in autumn, say, filled with russets and golds, and someone is leading me by the hand down a country lane (well, a lane by the side of my grandparents' house, on the outskirts of Belfast), where I enjoy a seasonal sensation (courtesy of William Brighty Rands):

> O I love to walk where the leaves lie dead,
> And hear their rustle beneath my tread!

Well, yes, indeed I do; but in the offing, and in a totally different order of evocation, is Keats's 'season of mists and mellow fruitfulness' which I will soon get by heart: its 'granary floor', its 'gathering swallows', 'Now in a wailful choir the small gnats mourn'. The poem washes over you and uplifts you at the same time, and its word-pictures set your senses a-humming. I think of the eleven-year-old Seamus Heaney at Anahorish Primary School in County Derry, rejoicing in the same poem: even though, as he says, 'the only line that was luminous then was "To bend with apples the mossed cottage trees", because my uncle had a small orchard where the old apple trees were sleeved in soft green moss'. I think of Heaney's Mossbawn childhood filled with ox-eye daisies and wild dandelions, with old rutted cart roads, 'Horses' collars lined with sweat-veined ticking', 'the annual bright booths of the fair at Toome'. All the trappings and rituals of country life.

The nearest I got to 'the country' was my paternal grandparents' gate lodge at the Malone Road end of Dunmurry Lane, where the recessed windows with orange geraniums planted in window boxes, the smell of straw and new-mown grass, the tea-table formally arranged for afternoon tea, distilled a sense of permanence and repose. I was a city child, a St James's/Falls Road child; though, as I've indicated, the seedy urban ambience of that part of Belfast was tempered by parks and fields, hedgerows and playgrounds, Milltown Row with its straggle of houses trailing down to the Bog Meadows, and, as a kind of counterpart, the Mountain Loney wending upwards to the well of pure spring water and the steep side of the Black Mountain with its bracken and boulders.

The Black Mountain held a special place in the affections of all of us in the St James's/Whiterock/Andersonstown area. It was the chief distinguishing feature of our particular neighbourhood. But another mountain loomed not too far away which was equally claimed as an emblem by the whole of Belfast. It was the Cave Hill. It presided over every part of the city. The bit of it known as 'Napoleon's Nose' lent itself to a unique personification. Viewing it from a vantage-point below, you could make out the form of a sleeper lying on his back, nose pointing skywards. Alice Milligan's poem 'Mountain Shapes', by virtue of the felicity of this image, places the Cave Hill above all other Irish hills:

> What hand of what Titan sculptor
> Smote the crags on the mountain vast?
> Made when the world was fashioned,
> Meant with the world to last,
> The glorious face of the Sleeper
> That slumbers above Belfast.

A benign presence, then, stationed over the city as a kind of guardian. Or, bearing in mind Belfast dissensions, it might be more apposite to think instead of a Gulliver figure chained down by ferocious Lilliputian troublemakers, while preserving a serene indifference to their machinations going on below.

Everyone in Belfast was familiar with the wondrous Cave Hill as a centre of holiday excursions and merry-making. Eggs were traditionally rolled down its slopes at Easter; and many young avid couples found the atmosphere of the place peculiarly conducive to concupiscence. A pleasure garden on the lower section, called Hazelwood, had an inviting tea room set up in a converted house, once the property of an Ebenezer Reid; and just along the way was the striking art deco ballroom known as the Floral Hall. Nearby you had Bellevue, home of the Belfast Zoo. Even as a child, I found the zoo rather dispiriting; it dismayed me to see the depressed animals far from their natural habitat. It was better to proceed upwards out of Hazelwood or Bellevue on sturdy legs towards the rugged summit and the famous spot by the topmost cave with the panoramic view of Ulster spread below. It was on this spot that Henry Joy McCracken, Theobald Wolfe Tone, Thomas Russell, Samuel Neilson, Robert Simms and one or two others had vowed to free Ireland and make it non-sectarian, or die in the attempt. The year was 1795, and the opportunity to act in accordance with their vow came three years later.

Some parts of Belfast have, or had, strong associations with 1798. Sugarhouse Entry, dating from 1678 and obliterated in the 1941 blitz, was the place where insurgents met to plan their course of action (in Peggy Barclay's Tavern there). A thatched house in Frederick Street (long demolished) was supposed to have sheltered Lord Edward

Fitzgerald when soldiers were hard on his heels (what was he doing in Belfast?). A counter in Kelly's Cellars – still in existence – likewise enabled Henry Joy McCracken to evade capture, and gained a permanent prestige for the inn on account of its rebel affiliation. And in Cornmarket, two months after the failure of the Rising, Henry Joy was hanged, by a curious twist, on land donated to the town by one of his ancestors; and passed into the pantheon of romantic Irish martyrs.

A 1798 episode concerning our own Hatchet Field was related to me when I was young. The field once held a cottage in its topmost corner. The cottage was gone in my day, but in it, I was told, had lived an old woman who, in her hundredth year, remembered hiding from the soldiers of General Nugent's army during the uprising. I think it was shyness, and not fear, that sent her scurrying for cover, for she was a Protestant and not a rebel. That was a pity. By the time I was six or seven I knew the difference, and I understood that it was more dashing to be aligned with dissent. I would have liked the Hatchet Field old woman's story to include the outwitting of these Redcoats, in the way girl members of the French Resistance in my weekly *School Friend* papers were constantly outwitting obtuse Nazi troopers ('Nina held her breath as the German raised the lid of the copper. Would he discover what was hidden under the washing?') And when I took to copious reading of school stories, it was the Fourth Form rebels, girls and boys alike, the risk-takers, opponents of injustice, those endowed with stupendous presence of mind in the face of an impending contretemps, who engaged my deepest assent ('Quickly then she whipped up the copy of the map. ... Only after that did she dive back into the crate. Just in time!').

I am five or six, and already books are more important to me than sweets or toys. But reading, as yet, is very much a matter of bits and pieces: an enraged dwarf here, a quaintly dressed orphan there, a twinkling star of indeterminate fabric in the sky. I am not equipped to grasp the magnitude of what's available, or to make choices; I just make do with whatever comes to hand, and count myself fortunate to inhabit a bookish home (relatively speaking). But I missed a lot. I can't now imagine what I'd have made of Winnie-the-Pooh, for example, had the book by A.A. Milne come my way at an appropriate moment (say, when I was three). As it happened, my view of that author was coloured irrevocably by the parodies I came across before I had read the originals – in particular, Richmal Crompton's splendid take on the entire Christopher Robin set-up (of which more later). And I remember an engaging couplet which goes: 'Hush, hush, nobody cares,/Christopher Robin has fallen downstairs.' I knew enough of the books by then to appreciate the parodies, but as for reading them ... that would have been the mental equivalent of scoffing an entire jar of honey in one go. I'm aware that Winnie-the-Pooh is a strong element in the typical middle-class English childhood of the mid-twentieth century, and indulgently regarded; and, as I say, if I had encountered the character in impressionable infancy, I might have been beguiled by the essence-of-stuffed-bear, Piglet and Eeyore along with everyone else. But I never read Milne until I was over twenty, when I couldn't see the Hundred Acre Wood for the twees – sorry, tweeness. On the subject of bears: I missed Mary Plain too, but I'm not sure that the activities of that little creature from Berne would have been much more to my liking. There's a talking-down-to-children quality about Mary Plain which I might have resented, for all the surface pleasantness of the little books in the series. (If I had to absorb a bear into my mental landscape, I'm glad it was Rupert.)

Beatrix Potter, now: there's a nursery absence to be lamented. No talking down in Beatrix Potter; just a bracing economy of child-size incident. And I wish someone had pointed me in the direction of Edward Ardizzone or Kathleen Hale: imagine being a child, and having Little Tim and his wonderfully depicted activities, or Orlando the Marmalade Cat with his benign and eventful family life, to keep your spirits raised! These are awash in charm, indeed, but charm of an inspiriting, never a cloying, kind. Imagine coming face to face with *The Little House in the Big Woods*, all Wisconsin witchery tempered by robustness – or opening John Masefield's *Box of Delights* and getting a full charge of mystery, snow, rat-villains, secret passages, a fabulous

Christmas tree, a midnight ride on a shining white pony.
And all conjured up with pantomimic vividness! But never
mind. A box of delights of my own, containing all the above
and more, much more, is waiting in the wings to expand my
reading horizons. 'The Public Library,' D.J.Enright wrote in
his collection *The Terrible Shears*, 'Handsomely stocked and
not used to excess/by the public...'. 'Bravo, England of the
Thirties!' he goes on; 'Your smallest, dullest town enclosed
alternatives/To littleness and dullness.' And Bravo, Northern
Ireland of the Fifties! And Dr Andrew Carnegie! And the
middle-aged female librarian of the Donegall Road Branch
Library in her faded blue overall! What matter if she took a
faintly censorious attitude to my insistence on borrowing the
early adventures of the Secret Seven: she stamped these, and
others, with her little rubber stamp in exchange for my clutch
of tickets, and allowed me to carry them away, only indulging
in a sniff of disapproval on account of my low tastes.

She must have been slightly gratified that I was there at
all: this library, like Dennis Enright's, was not overused. But
I at least was soon an habituée. Taken to the place by my
mother, once I had attained six years and become proficient
in reading, led by the hand up the marble staircase to the
children's section on the first floor and introduced to the
concept of books for the taking, I was face to face with a kind of
sustenance I'd been craving nearly from the word go. I might
say, if it hadn't been for the presence of restraining adults, on
that first day, I'd have flung myself on the gloriously laden

bookshelves and gathered up their contents by the armful ....
But it won't do. The histrionic gesture is not in keeping with
the finely honed sense of rapture and wonderment pervading
the dusty room with its ingrained book-aroma, the pleasing
Watt and Tulloch red-brick library building, the cries of a
rag-and-bone man in the street below. Besides, at six, I was
a self-contained and fairly undemonstrative child; only my
mother would have known that what I was experiencing
was something like an onrush of anticipation and pleasure
in a peculiarly heightened form .... No, it's better to stick
with Enright's echo of Peter Porter's 'Oft have I travelled in
the realms of gold,/For which I thank the Paddington and
Westminster Public Libraries...'. That's about the gist of it.
Or, with Ian Sansom, I might claim that 'what I remember
[is] not my own childhood at all but a kind of composite
red-brick and mahogany Carnegie Library childhood, made
up of my own and other people's memories and fantasies and
imaginations'.[1]

---

[1] Ian Sansom Website: 'On Prefaces'.

2. THE BOX OF DELIGHTS

I learned to use the Public Library,
that red-brick haven which Carnegie built.
In bed, at table, I read avidly,
for in our house there was no blame or guilt
because 'you stuck your nose in some old book'
John Hewitt, 'Reading'

I SOMETIMES ENVISAGE MY DOTAGE as a state in which I will be for ever attempting to board a double-decker trolley bus going up the Donegall Road from Shaftesbury Square, and alighting at the stop directly opposite Number 551, my childhood home. It was a route I travelled every day when I was nine or ten, coming home from school at Aquinas Hall, having first caught another bus down the Malone Road – 'the faubourg Malone', as a local satirist had it. It was a journey from affluent seclusion into seedy congestion. As I stood at the stop near the junction of Bradbury Place and the bottom end of the Donegall Road, I was right beside an old-fashioned barber's shop called Cahoon's, and running down the side of this shop was an exceedingly narrow lane, McFarland's Court, in which five or six white-washed, two-storey houses were jammed together in hapless contiguity. At an angle to the main row, at the far end of the lane, was a further house with possibly the narrowest frontage I have ever seen. It was a mystery to me how its inhabitants managed to squeeze in and out, or found enough space to sit in comfort once they were inside. It was a bad case of inadequate accommodation. However, a fairly substantial, double-fronted house, separated from Cahoon's by the entrance to McFarland's Court, faced the Donegall Road and presented a more seemly aspect, pointing up the niceties of social gradation. Somewhat subliminally, I enjoyed the multifariousness of all this housing muddle.

But of far more interest to me was a very distinctive building I could see from the bus stop, about a hundred yards away on an upward slope. (It can still be seen, though everything else I've referred to above has long been obliterated.) It was architecturally pleasing and seemed at odds with its rough hinterland. It was red-brick, Edwardian, foursquare, functional and decorative all at once. It was the dearly beloved, well-appointed Carnegie Library on the Donegall Road.

Often I would go straight out again after arriving home from school, and catch a bus back down the road to the library. I'd be in a highly focused state of mind, my entire being concentrated on locating some outstanding opus with a title like *Bookworm the Mystery-Solver* or *The Seventh Pig*. The library was my equivalent of the young carbohydrate-addict's corner sweet shop. Without it, I'd have led a curtailed life in a tedium of fiction-deprivation. So bravo, again, Andrew Carnegie – even if my part of the library was only an adjunct to the crucial service the philanthropist's enterprise offered. Its essential purpose was to foster self-improvement among the working classes, not to cater to juvenile bookish cupidity. But there it was – and there I was, fortunately born at a time when its existence was taken for granted. Since before the First World War, the needs of proletarian Belfast readers had been acknowledged and met. The Donegall Road branch, no less than its counterparts elsewhere in the city, was a fixture in that particular dicey locality. It included Sandy Row in its catchment area, along with the welter of jam-packed side-streets radiating out from this infamous thoroughfare, whose inhabitants probably didn't count the availability of books among their primary needs. Apart from Robert Harbinson, that is – though oddly, Harbinson's vivid account of growing up alert to everything else in Sandy Row and environs (*No Surrender*, 1960) does not mention the library. *No Surrender* has a lot about dangerous play by the railway lines, the tuberculosis clinic, the Bog Meadows, exorbitant Orangeism, the discomforts and resources of back-street living, but nothing at all about the book repository nearly on the author's doorstep. Clearly, Robert Harbinson was one of those bookish children who never took to children's books – only the Masefield poem 'Cargoes' gained his approval, it seems – but waited for adulthood to equip him with the means to absorb his preferred type of reading. At nine or ten he was too busy playing with tinker children in the Bog Meadows, or joyously anticipating 'the Twelfth', to take time out for Rockfist Rogan or Biggles. At least, if he ever found himself drawn to these fictional supermen, they are not among the features of his childhood he wishes to perpetuate.

It was different for those of us for whom fiction, unexalted and colourful fiction, was a kind of life's-breath. Like Elizabeth Bowen, we 'inhaled' it, thrived on it and internalised it. And the public library was our Elysium. Here I am, six years old, instantly attuned to the concept of book-borrowing, and about to make the acquaintance of the Secret Seven, whose attraction to the strange, peculiar and queer – the adjectives are Enid Blyton's – seems to me an obvious way to make the most of the world and its goings-on. The meeting place of this enterprising group is a shed at the bottom of Peter and Janet's garden, its *raison d'être* is to get a handle on any local mysteries, and its success rate, in accordance with the principles of wish-fulfilment, puts the police to shame.

The first adventure of the Secret Seven proper involves a queer carry-on at an old dark house whose sole occupant is a bad-tempered caretaker wielding a big stick. A strong aversion to what he – not without cause – calls pestering, interfering children animates this character. Not a whit dismayed by his threats or his stick, the law-upholding Seven keep an eye on the place, spot a couple of miscreants stowing an agitated racehorse in the cellar, and promptly restore the horse's trust in humanity by speaking kindly to it: well, two of them do this, having undertaken the hazardous extrication of the horse from the house, while the others stand on guard outside disguised as snowmen. These interesting activities take place in the middle of a winter's night, while the parents of the Seven – we may suppose – snore tranquilly at home, in happy ignorance of their offsprings' profitable imprudence.

I think this Blyton episode was the first adventure story I carried home from the Donegall Road library, where I felt it had been waiting for me, the ideal reader. I took it all in. I loved the mildly wintry setting, with accompanying illustrations featuring scarves and overcoats, the ritual accoutrements of password and badge, the good work accomplished by the civic-minded Seven. It didn't bother me that Blyton had failed to provide her characters with distinguishing marks more noteworthy than their names, or that difficulties in the way of their crime-busting projects were surmounted with staggering ease. The overblown outcome was part of the magic. And magic there was, though without the smallest *frisson* of the numinous. In Blyton's hands, neither the atmosphere nor the story-line was at all elaborated. Things were kept on an exceedingly superficial plane, which at the same time was oddly satisfying. Other forms of literary nourishment might, and did, work at a deeper level, but for high-definition, unnuanced entertainment, Blyton (for a time at least) reigned unopposed.

Before I had finished with Blyton, I'd devoured almost every word of her prodigious output, not excluding the Biblical retellings, Brer Rabbit or the Arabian Nights. (I only drew the line at Noddy; I was probably too old for them, by the time these infantile episodes began to appear. The title of an early strip book, *Noddy is Very Silly*, summed up my attitude to that particular series.) But it was the adventure and mystery stories – the main series – that furnished (for me) the ultimate in delight. I soon graduated from the Secret Seven to the Famous Five, and, with the opening book, was guided through the excitements of a riveting holiday adventure, complete with private island, treasure map and regurgitated wreck. There's a ruined castle on the island too, in whose dungeons two of the Five are imprisoned by stop-at-nothing thieves in a desperate rush to get their hands on a cache of lost gold. They are wasting their time, of course; as an early reviewer of Blyton, Eileen Colwell, pointed out in 1948, no wrongdoers stand a chance when confronted by intrepid English children wearing shorts and sandals, having right on their side and never hesitating to launch themselves into the crumbling shaft of a long-abandoned well.

Ten or twelve of these wonderful, enveloping adventure stories would have been available to me, before I outgrew the series. Indeed, I still have my original copy of *Five on a Hike Together*, dated 1951 and inscribed by me in uncouth handwriting. This particular title must have come as a Christmas present, since I owned it, while most of the 'Fives' were on loan from the library. Christmas, of course, was the time when delectable piles of Blytons, 'Just William' stories and others would mysteriously appear at the end of my bed during the night, and lead to a waking-up state of book-induced bliss. *Hilary's Island* – ah! *Jane the Unlucky* – oh! I think it must have been around this time that the book-as-object got embedded in my consciousness as a supercharged shibboleth: in other words, a collector was being made (I'll get back later to the subject of collecting). In the early days, though, I just wanted to read the story, and it didn't much matter what form it came in. I wouldn't have known a first edition from a *Reader's Digest* abridgement, library bindings didn't bother me, and a paperback Martin Clifford was certainly, in my view, as desirable an acquisition as a bound volume of original *Gems*. But I was laying the ground for a future susceptibility to the full evocative effect of the book itself: dust-jacket, illustrations and all. There'd come a time when every felicitous association of the earliest reading experience would come into play.

It was standard practice at the time for public libraries to rebind their books, discarding dust-covers; and possibly because of this I acquired an idea that books were truer to themselves when detached from their wrappers, and that my own small collection looked better on the shelf with no untidy or trumpery jackets to detract from its tasteful plainness. (I have had to replace the lot of them since.) But one or two jackets survived, because even at the time I could see they upheld and enriched the atmosphere of the story. If I had to put my finger on a single, quintessential Blyton, for example, I think I would opt for *The Castle of Adventure* with the Stuart Tresilian cover embodying all the charm and exhilaration of 1940s writing for children: the slightly muted greens and blues and reds of the jerseys worn by the venturesome quartet; the sense of movement and expectancy pervading the image; the eponymous castle looming appropriately in the background, the twisted thorn tree, the ragged, barefoot local girl Tassie with her shoes strung round her neck. Add Kiki, the remarkable parrot perched on one boy's shoulder, Button the adorable fox cub draped around the shoulders of the other boy, the sturdy girls with their curly brown hair and outdoor élan, and you know you're in for a session of enthralment. Well, you do if you're nine years old and eager to be thrilled to the core by imaginary dangers in underground rooms, secret passages, animated suits of armour and a climax involving Secret Service business, a villain called Scar-Neck and an opportune landslide.

I had my own copy of this marvellous book and I kept it, and its jacket, for years. What eventually became of the book and the jacket I don't know. The copy in my library at present was once the property of a Judy Browne, according to an inscription in juvenile handwriting on the front endpaper, and she lived in a house called Wentworth in Hertfordshire .... It's a far cry from the Donegall Road with its factories and pubs and greyhound owners wearing duncher caps, and innumerable side streets of workaday terraces: banal then, but stamped with a kind of poignancy now. And its library, in whose first-floor cornucopia the majority of the 'Fives', the 'Adventure' series, the 'Rockingdown Mystery' series, the 'Find-Outers' and the 'Spiggy Holes' crew were pounced on by me. Once I'd got them home – according to season – I'd either sit in a deckchair in the garden, or curl up in a rust-coloured armchair in the front room, and wrap myself in delectation and mystery. Francis Spufford, in *The Child that Books Built* (his compelling account of juvenile reading and its effects) comments on the nearly palpable sense of absorption about the place when someone in the house gets lost in a book. A special kind of hush, his mother calls it, a reading silence. 'My seven-year-old self,' he explains, 'had become about as absent as a present person could be.' This is true for all of us. For the duration of the story, you are somewhere else entirely, in every sense except the physical, imprisoned in an old house on a cliff that once belonged to smugglers, wearing a sunsuit in a heatwave in a pretty English village and outwitting a stupid policeman named Goon, solving the mystery while he stands scratching his head in bewilderment, or tumbling down a rabbit hole on a faraway, windswept Scottish island, with a gang of crooks in the offing and a parrot and a pair of puffins for company. ... I'm aware that a degree of absorption is a function of reading, any reading: but what I'm trying to describe goes beyond an ordinary engagement with the narrative. What separates the fiction addict from the occasional reader is equivalent to the gulf between an acorn and an oak tree, or a rocking horse and a living pony.

This submitting of yourself to the flow of the story is a voluntary process, of course; or at least it starts out that way, before the words on the page come to constitute a heightened reality, keeping you up in the clouds until it's all over, unless you're brought down to earth prematurely, by being shaken or shouted at. If you're left to read on and on until the end, you emerge from a trancelike state feeling either invigorated, or mildly let down by the denouement, as the case may be. The crucial factor here, as ever, is atmosphere: the atmosphere generated by the author, which pulls or repels you, to varying degrees. And for those most fervent and persuasible readers – children under the age of twelve, say – the atmosphere of a story will gain in piquancy once a certain amount of time has been lived through, and the book in question has become a fragment of a rapidly receding past. Often, though not invariably, the atmosphere of a book will transcend its actual content: there are dangers in approaching, in middle age, some colourful piece of claptrap that appeased a craving for the unfolding story, when you were ten. You may be fearfully disillusioned. I will come back later to a few of the reasons why some children's books can stand rereading, while others can't; with the latter (which includes the bulk of Blyton, alas) it's the silliness of the plots which exacerbates the adult sensibility. But it is none the less possible to retain a pleasant sense of the atmosphere of a story, irrespective of its bogus or preposterous drift; and added on top of that, you have the atmosphere of the time when no extraneous evaluation got between you, the reader, and an unadulterated engrossment. To evoke all this to the highest degree, it is necessary to own the actual volume, in its original form: which is one reason why many of us avid childhood readers become collectors.

Of course, most sensible adults would no more think of sitting down to read a children's book than heading for the seaside with a bucket and spade. It is not only our fate, as Elizabeth Bowen has it, but our business to lose innocence, 'and once we have lost it it is futile to attempt a picnic in Eden'. Yes, true. But some of us contrive to have it both ways. We read those childhood books – those that remain rereadable, that is – but manufacture all kinds of rationalisations and justifications for the practice, of which the most obvious is literary curiosity, usually in the form of research into the populist culture of the past. We proclaim ourselves connoisseurs of storybook absurdities, which chimes with a blasé sensibility, the prerogative of age. The secret agenda, the wish to propel oneself backwards into a cosier and more dynamic dimension, isn't much bruited about. Of course, the enjoyment to be derived from bygone children's stories is only, and inevitably, an extremely watered-down version of the euphoria they once engendered. But then, you have to take into account the extra mnemonic charge due to all the accretions garnered along the way: so you may end in the odd position, with your *Secret of Spiggy Holes*, of experiencing a diminished and intensified effect simultaneously.

Indeed, you don't even have to read the book to gain a strong mnemonic charge: sometimes it's enough to have the Biggles or William with the Thomas Henry cover or the row of Nancy Brearys in front of you.... And then, though they may have started out from an equivalent plane of addiction in childhood, a distinction needs to be made between the grown-up juvenile-reading-aficionado, for whom any shoddy reprint or tattered popular edition will do the trick, and the thoroughgoing collector whose pursuit of the ultimate copy – the dust-jacketed, flawless, unsurpassable copy – is somehow tied up with the fullest retrieval of the initial state of reading rapture which underlies the whole business.

The collecting impulse, of course, is no doubt rooted in some psychological quirk connected to a powerful formative experience, and what it attaches itself to is a matter of personal preference: vintage door-stops, as it may be, or railway posters or the works of the rhyming weavers of Antrim and Down. Whatever form it takes, it – like gambling, to which it is related – can easily get out of hand, burgeoning in all directions, filling your home with objects whose function or desirability is a mystery to everyone else. Why would anyone *want* a room full of bakelite wirelesses? It does not matter, as P.G. Wodehouse[1] said on the subject, 'what a man collects; if Nature has given him the collector's mind, he will become

---

[1] P.G. Wodehouse, *Something Fresh* (1915).

a fanatic on the subject of whatever collection he sets out to make.' He goes on:

> Mr Peters had collected dollars, [and] he began to collect scarabs with precisely the same enthusiasm. He would have become just as enthusiastic about butterflies, or old china, if he had turned his thoughts to them, but it chanced that what he had taken up was the collecting of the scarab, and it gripped him more and more as the years went on.

Collecting, as Mr Peters went in for it, says P.G. Wodehouse, 'resembles the drink habit. It begins as an amusement, and ends as an obsession.' I can testify to the truth of this observation. Never having collected dollars, or pounds, but fixing my sights on books instead, I have sometimes (metaphorically speaking) gone barefoot to accommodate my addiction. When it comes to books, too, the original genre that sparked the whole thing off is liable to get added to by connected genres, so that you end up obsessively on the trail of books you never read, or would have wanted to read.

There was a period in my life – between the ages of fourteen or fifteen, say, and twenty-five – when children's books held not the slightest interest for me. Then, one day – it was midsummer – I happened to be in a street market in Brighton, when my eye was caught by a book on a junk stall: *The Luckiest Girl in the School*, it was, by Angela Brazil, with a cover featuring three sporty schoolgirls with picturesque hair-dos and businesslike hockey sticks. In that instant, the notion came into my head that it might be amusing to amass a collection of old girls' books like this one, with their wonderfully decorative bindings and egregious approach to school-storytelling. Fishing out half-a-crown to pay for the book, I persuaded myself I was buying it with a sociological object in mind, and *not* because I had never shaken off a hankering after perpetual juvenility. A new kind of feminism was in the air, and I was thinking vaguely about applying a few of its tenets to a study of girls' fiction (this project was completed, in due course, once I'd joined forces with Mary Cadogan and collaborated with her on *You're a Brick, Angela!*[2]). But it was something odder than that, and more deeply submerged, that made the book irresistible to me – and *not* as a recovered childhood treasure. At eight or nine, I had tried Angela Brazil (I tried whatever was available), but she never came within an ace of meeting my upbeat requirements. I turned up my nose at her old-fashioned airs, perhaps without due consideration. If, as it seemed to me then, a miasma of fustiness and inertness pervaded her stories, it was nothing to that afflicting Dorothea Moore, say, or E.L. Haverfield, Amy le Feuvre, Mrs Ewing, Mrs Molesworth, or – horrors – L.T. Meade, with her unspeakably dismal *World of Girls*. Of course, it would have been the 1950s' Brazil reprints that came my way, and not the first editions in their full Edwardian glory. Not that I would have appreciated those either at the time; nothing mattered then but the story,

[2] Published by Victor Gollancz in 1976.

and associations accruing to the books because of their period colouring would have passed me by.

Even in the 1950s, I am sure, the books of Brazil could hardly be read by anyone in the way the author intended; and for those of us under ten at the time this meant they weren't much read at all. You had to have acquired a certain knowingness to approach them in an Arthur Marshall spirit of levity: though we did pick out a few examples of passé alacrity, my uppity little friends and I, making ourselves fall about in fits of merriment. 'Did you have jolly hols?' we might ask one another, to which the correct reply was, 'Absolutely ripping, thanks.' Or: 'The old coll. looks no end. It's so smart and spanky now, one hardly knows it.' 'Smart and spanky' became one of our catchphrases. This was the only form of entertainment we were able to extract from Angela Brazil, and we missed a lot of her wilder excesses of spiffing schoolgirlishness. Well, a term of approbation such as 'Miss Jones is a stunt, as jinky as you like', would not have suited any of the pasty-faced nuns who taught us. Nor did our everyday friendships 'flame to red heat', unlike that of Aldred and Mabel in an early Brazil story. No, I was into my thirties before the full impact of the Brazil oeuvre became available to me. I was then equipped to relish the whole of it as a source of divertissement and a period piece, and also to give its author credit for the new departure it undoubtedly was in its day. In 1912 or thereabouts, the Brazil breeziness came as a welcome riposte to the staidness of earlier authors working in the genre.

Adventure stories were more to our liking, when we were ten. Indeed, those key words, 'adventure', 'secret' and 'mystery' encapsulate the fascination of all those hordes of stories featuring policemen's little helpers (even if the policemen weren't aware of their existence until the final page, when the crime was cleared up following the children's efforts, and the villains handed over to justice on a plate). As far as I and my reading friends were concerned, a side-effect of all this mystery-solving was to ram into our heads a distorted idea of what was possible in actuality and what was not. We went adventuring, over and over, with the Silent Three and the Famous Five, secure in the belief that comparable excitements awaited us in our normal lives, just around the corner. Steeped in the doings of hooded avengers of assorted wrongs, unjust expulsions, false accusations and the like, we considered the crypt at midnight or the lonely cove a perfectly suitable meeting place to plan a retaliatory strategy. We were proxy mystery-solvers, looking forward to the real thing; though as time went by and no solvable burglaries or strange disappearances occurred to require our attention in the vicinity of Slemish Way or La Salle Drive in west Belfast, we were left bemoaning the scarcity of real-life adventures on the Secret Seven model. Our appetite for the fictional version remained unabated, though.

Looking round my bookshelves the other day, I was struck by a thought: so that's what I've been up to all these years, going all out to recreate the contents of the children's section of the Donegall Road Library in Belfast, c.1952. Here in front of me are the blessed Blytons, in all their heady variety, from *Six Cousins at Mistletoe Farm* to the highly dubious Mr Pinkwhistle (*Mr Pinkwhistle Interferes* is a title that might raise an eyebrow or two today). Here is Malcolm Saville with his thrilling Lone Pine series, a series beginning in 1943 with German spies popping up all over the Long Mynd Mountain in Shropshire only to meet defeat at the hands of some remarkable children; the anarchic activities of headstrong Jane Turpin as related by Evadne Price; anodyne Mabel Esther Allan and outrageous Rita Coatts with her plucky redheads and flying escapes and hands reaching out of nowhere to clutch the heroine's arm; and a good deal more. The collecting habit which has dominated much of my adult life can be traced back to that pivotal library and the middle part of the twentieth century, though I have improved on the library's rexine bindings by holding out for original dust-jackets.

Collecting, as I've indicated, is a passion not easily explicable to anyone who doesn't share it. Once word of it gets out, you may risk being labelled eccentric, at the very least; but I don't think many of us children's-books enthusiasts would go as far to conceal our obsession as the distinguished old gentleman in the J.I.M. Stewart story, 'Teddy Lester's Schooldays', who behaved so surreptitiously with regard to his fancy for old boys' books that he got himself suspected of pornography. I am sure that most of us collectors aren't odd at all, this one quirk aside. We're not retarded or stuck in the past, thank you very much, and perfectly well able to distinguish between *Maisie's Discovery* and *What Maisie Knew*. We don't attribute the creation of a marmalade cat to Virginia Woolf, or imagine that *Autumn Journal* has anything to do with a diary kept by a character in *Autumn Term*. We know *The Doings of Dorothea* do not take place in an imaginary town called Middlemarch.

By the time I was seven or eight, I was trusted to make my own way to the library, and soon (as I've said) this became an almost daily practice, after school. It just entailed stepping on to a double-decker bus at the stop only yards from our front gate, and then alighting from a similar bus on the opposite side of the road on the return journey, carrying my current selection of reading material. ...I must have cut an odd figure at the far end of the Donegall Road, with my skimpy plaits, posh royal blue Aquinas Hall blazer, Clarke's sandals and white ankle socks; but no one paid any attention to me, as far as I recall. Urchins at my own end of the road were more likely to go in for name-calling on account of the blazer, which seemed to get up their proletarian noses. Actually, I wore it because I had to, not to lord it over anyone, particularly over local elementary school pupils. We certainly weren't a moneyed or pretentious family, and whatever surplus income we had probably went on the fees – four and a half guineas a term – at my convent preparatory school on the Malone Road. The royal blue uniform on top of that would have used up whatever meagre clothes allowance was alloted to me.

Possibly I escaped the jeers of backstreet contemporaries down the Donegall Road because I stuck to the main road; I never walked down Utility Street past the Cripples' Institute with Eureka Street behind it, or savoured the smell of newly baked bread from the bakery in nearby Bentham Street. My whole attention was focused on furthering my vocation as a reader, not on making any foolhardy foray into dubious territory. Like every Belfast child above the age of reason, I was well-schooled in the principles of sectarian expediency. Within a stone's throw of Sandy Row – if anyone had grasped the implication of my Aquinas Hall blazer, which admittedly was unlikely – I'd have had a Papist despicability to answer for, on top of acting Miss Lah-di-dah. Inside the library, though, with its punctilious hush and rays of dusty sunlight slanting through the windows high up in the walls above the rows of bookshelves, you were safe from any form of juvenile harassment. The unspoken agreement was that any child borrower admitted into the select upper room would guarantee to remain on its best behaviour; if not, you'd be ejected as fast as Mickey Mouse from a cannon, and a lot more ignominiously. If cheerful unruliness was what you craved, you had to make do with it at second-hand, and find it in some of the books.

In that library, for instance, I made the acquaintance of William Brown, in whom the state of being eleven years old gets its ultimate expression. I came on William by chance, and a very merry chance it was. It's possible that I was drawn into the stories by Thomas Henry's jaunty illustrations as I flicked through one of the books. I might have been struck by the expectant expression on William's agreeably rough-hewn face as he stands in a bad posture with his socks falling down, while some glorious piece of mischief flashes into his mind. And the stories were not a let-down. William's zest for disruption is joyously elaborated, as the author, Richmal Crompton, directs the terrible child through a series of intricate mishaps ('William's Busy Day'; 'William Makes Things Hum'). It's not that he is ill-meaning – on the contrary – just that any benevolent scheme initiated by William tends to go spectacularly awry. ' "I wanted to *help*.' " ... ' "But William ... how did you think it would help *anyone* to say that Ethel had epilepsy and consumption?'"

Robert and Ethel, foils to perfection, are the languid older brother and sister whose role is to reel from repeated assaults on their sensibility innocently carried out by William. ' "You'd think he wouldn't be allowed to go around ruining people's lives and – and spoiling their bicycles.'" This bitter observation comes from Robert as William, with blackened face and doormat pinned to his shoulders, inadvertently puts a spoke in yet another of his brother's budding romances. William, full-blooded opponent of tedium and decorum, instructed all of us restricted readers in the ways of irrepressible antics and jovial self-assertion. The outcome of his activities had us either smiling in satisfaction at the wonderful symmetry of the resolution, or positively rolling about in an outbreak of hilarity. I wasn't close to eleven myself when I discovered William, and I certainly wasn't a boy in the Home Counties with a trio of fellow outlaws at my command and an Old Barn to plan peculiar undertakings in ('William Sells the Twins'; 'William Clears the Slums'). But I knew I'd fit well into William's world, with my readiness to engage in any doughty enterprise (in theory at least: it wasn't often put to the test), fondness for dogs and ability to shin up lamp posts. I blocked out my girlish aversion to insects, secret swotting proclivities and kowtowing to adult dictates.

William's articulate remoteness from grown-ups' concerns is the factor that creates an abundance of social comedy; and unbeknownst to myself, courtesy of Richmal Crompton, I was getting a good grounding in this aspect of the English comic tradition, as well as gaining some insights into the social history of the period between the wars. (Though the William books continued to appear right up until the end of the nineteen sixties, they had somehow lost their vim in the post-war years.) Years later, I was reading for the first time the opening section of Louis MacNeice's 'Autumn Journal', when an inappropriate picture formed in my mind. MacNeice is mapping a vanishing England, reposeful and distant and more than a bit stuffy, with its

...ramps of shaven lawn where close-clipped yew
Insulates the lives of retired generals and admirals
And the spyglasses hung in the hall and the prayer-books
    ready in the pew, ...

And the spinster sitting in a deck-chair picking up stitches
Not raising her eyes to the noise of the 'planes that pass
Northward from Lee-on-Solent. Macrocarpa and cypress
And roses on a rustic trellis and mulberry trees
And bacon and eggs in a silver dish for breakfast
And all the inherited assets of bodily ease ....

and I felt I knew this territory, if only at second-hand. Just for
a moment, it didn't seem too great a distortion of the spirit
of the poem to superimpose over MacNeice's reminders of a
bygone stability and tranquillity, a force of nature rampaging
in the shrubbery complete with wild Indian headdress and
tomahawk, and bent on joyful mayhem. William Brown, whose
encounters with retired generals and admirals and knitting
spinsters ginger up one piece of fusty protocol after another.
All right, I knew I was jamming together two incompatible
modes of apprehension, but before I had entered completely
into the mood of the poem, the association was irresistible.

Besides, I believed I had some justification for monkeying
with MacNeice. Was he not as much a product of the
North of Ireland as I was – born in Belfast, accustomed to
hooting sirens and the clang of trams, with a family home
(eventually) at 77 Malone Road, next door to my old school?
I took a proprietary interest in Louis MacNeice. Of course,
for him, the North spelled bleakness and repression, and
Belfast in particular came in for a drubbing at his hands.
'Belfast! Belfast! City of smoke and dust.' This was the chant
declaimed by MacNeice and his sister, as children, saying

goodbye to the horrible city as the train from York Street Station bore them homewards towards Carrickfergus, the castle, the residential houses and the good sea air.

I relished the pungency of MacNeice's disparagement of his birthplace: the street children with their games of hopscotch and marbles on wet pavements, the rich families' lawns and sagging tennis nets, the tubercular unemployed assembling at back-street corners; factionalism, philistinism, commercialism and bad weather. And on top of all that, the banners and bunting proclaiming some antiquated affiliation. Oh yes, indeed. But I also relished the place itself, the smoke and fog, the rainy streets, the interesting courts and alleyways, Pottinger's Entry, Kelly's Cellars with their historical associations, the mountain with the Hatchet Field engraved on its surface, eternally visible from my bedroom window.

This bedroom is also a room to ingest fiction in. Reading in bed is an incomparable resource, an escape from the chores and headaches and humiliations of juvenile everyday life. Here I am cocooned and comfortable, and immeasurably entertained to boot. A cache of library books is arranged before me on the blue satin quilted eiderdown. A mug of steaming cocoa sits on a bedside table. It's not yet time to put out the light, even though the streetlamps outside are casting a mellowing glow on the wet pavements and dank front gardens of the Donegall Road, and rowdy groups of boys and girls are passing at intervals bound for some homespun shebeen. And what is keeping me awake, more intensely awake, I would think, than I am during the day? 'The Case of the Emril Ring', perhaps, or 'The Blue Tulle Poke Bonnet', featuring intractable Jane Turpin, rumbustious girlhood's answer to William Brown. Jane, of the angelic appearance and tearaway disposition, appeases some craving in all of us to be constantly on the go. Like William's, the pickles Jane lands in have a way of coming out right. Her sterling hyperactivity is presented as a glorious counterblast to adult weariness and conservatism, along with juvenile tale-bearing and smugness. Jane's primary adversary in the stories by Evadne Price is the vicar's scrawny daughter Amelia Tweeddale – Soppy Melia to her contemporaries – whose goody-goody and underhand ways are pilloried without mercy. It's *de rigueur* for Melia to arrive at a striking comeuppance:

> ... a naked figure in a gas-mask, smelling of pungent mustard and onions and thickly coated in oil and some other filthy foreign body, fell through the French windows into the drawing-room on to Miss Baldock's beautiful Persian carpet. 'Amelia!' screamed Mrs Tweeddale.

There's a vision to fall asleep with. For all of us properly spirited and above-board eight-year-olds – in our own view anyway – Soppy Melia comes into the obnoxious-infant category, along with satin-suited Georgie in a William episode and the Christopher Robin clone, also a creation of Richmal Crompton, whose private tantrums belie his public image. Melia is born to be reviled, just as Jane, cavorting about the village accompanied by Popeye the Pup and her henchmen Pug and Chaw (Percival and Charles, according to their mothers), elicits cheer after cheer from all of us ardent readers.

Merry upheaval is one thing, and engaging decorum another. I was never much of a one for career novels, apart from those highlighting a girl reporter or sleuth, which propelled them into a different category as far as I was concerned. But the cornerstone of all the career stories, Noel Streatfeild's *Ballet Shoes*, struck a chord with the part of myself that approved of order, hard work, a fairytale blueprint and a sedate London setting. 'The Fossil sisters lived in the Cromwell Road.' Actually, they aren't sisters and their name isn't Fossil. They've been garnered as infants by an eccentric old gentleman, a one-time fossil-hunter, and deposited, one by one, on the lap of the blithe old gentleman's great-niece Sylvia. The ex-fossil-hunter then takes off on his travels for the next twelve years, leaving the newly configured small family, including Nana, to fend for itself. How the Fossils make out in the absence of GUM (Great-Uncle Matthew) forms the substance of the story. They are talented children. Pauline is destined to be an actress of note and Posy a famous ballerina, while mechanically minded Petrova achieves her own brand of distinction, shaping up for a flying future. In the meantime, there is that golden-hued London of 1931, velvet frocks from Harrods and walks to the Victoria and

Albert Museum, Cook in the kitchen and Nana in the nursery, old-time social arrangements unthreatened and good fortune assured for the deserving. Irresistible!

Christmas has come around again, and this year I am seven. One of my presents is a thick, green-backed book entitled *A Staircase of Stories*, which begins with an easy-to-read item about an old woman and her pig. I read this story, and the next one, and the one after that, without succumbing to undue rejoicing. I understand the purpose of the volume, the idea being that you should progress through it step-by-step, tackling increasingly demanding stories or extracts from novels as your intellect becomes equal to them. But the well-meaning editors of the *Staircase* are up against the instincts of a fiction-addict, who cannot countenance having a book full of stories in her hands and choosing to put some aside for future consumption. Never mind if some are supposed to be too old for me. I read on and on, even if I can't claim to have devoured every word: some stories hold more immediate appeal than others, as collections of pieces by different authors will. I am not enthralled by the Fairchild family with their broken heads resulting from disobedience; and a spider called Anensi fails to rivet my attention.

From the *Staircase*, though, I derived an enhanced appreciation of long-ago quaintness, quaintness which resolved itself into a series of vignettes: Nathaniel Hawthorne's 'Snow Child' with a flock of snowbirds alighting on her fingertips, the upright, and upland, Swiss peasants of 'Margot and the Golden Fish'. (A colour illustration by M.D. Spooner increased the fascination of this worthy piece.) Acceptable reading material, I began to understand, covered a wider range than the stuff I was used to. The stories and episodes I preferred, though, weren't located in some immemorial dreamworld but took place closer to home and closer to the present – well, in so far as either can be applied with accuracy to Edwardian England. 'Pomona in London' demurely taking tea with a courteous old military gentleman is one; and 'Muriel Goes to a Party', a mildly humorous take on social embarrassment, the other. Muriel, a little girl staying with her aunt in London, is invited to a party and goes to the wrong one. Blundering out of a dark street and into a house with light streaming from its open door, she finds herself among a throng of glittering guests, none of whom is wearing fancy dress. Poor Muriel cuts a queer figure with her night-cap, pointy hat and besom, and flees in mortification. But all ends well. Mabel Quiller-Couch wrote the story, Anne Anderson drew Muriel dressed as The Old Woman who Swept the Cobwebs out of the Sky, and I enjoyed the tiny contretemps. What I enjoyed more, though, was the sense of decorous gaiety, the tall elaborate houses and horse-drawn carriages, the freezing night, the silks and muslins of fashionable young people.

Long before I ever went to London, I knew its permutations from a raggedy East End hullabaloo to a Kensington propriety. I knew its blitzed quarters, one-time streets of stately houses reduced to rubble and overgrown with bindweed and willow-herb. I knew the daunting exclusive shops of Regent Street and Piccadilly, and the barrows of cheery and incorrigible costermongers. I understood the way London fogs and smogs fostered shady goings-on. But I never accompanied the 'Psammead' quartet on their walks along the Kentish Town Road, or into the dubious courts and alleyways near Ludgate Circus and Fetter Lane; or, for that matter, journeyed with them on their flying carpet towards imaginary predicaments, all at a satisfyingly ludicrous remove from the world as they knew it. Chance ordained that E. Nesbit, at least for the time being, would remain a closed book to me.

It was my own fault. When I was seven or eight, a school friend came in one day bursting with enthusiasm for *Five Children and It*. I'd be bowled over by it, she told me, it was hilarious: I should rush to the library and get it out, once she'd returned the copy she was reading to the Donegall Road branch. But, fatally, I asked her what was meant by 'It'. 'It' was a fairy – an unusual, fractious and funny fairy, she assured me; but the damage was done. I turned up my nose at 'fairy'. The word carried infantile connotations. I had outgrown fairies, thank you very much. Enid Blyton's Silky was a thing of the past. So I missed the Psammead at a proper age through sticking to a foolish prejudice. I should have listened to my dark-haired friend from the Lisburn Road; she was older than me, and possessed of more discriminating ways. As it was, another fifteen years would pass before I opened that book by E.Nesbit and read,

> The children stood round the hole in a ring, looking at the creature they had found. It was worth looking at. Its eyes were on long horns like a snail's eyes, and it could move them in and out like telescopes; it had ears like a bat's ears, and its tubby body was shaped like a spider's and covered with thick soft fur. ... It looked scornfully at Jane's hat as it spoke.

With some books you are drawn in, like a salmon getting a scent of a feed, and just as quickly hooked: though with consequences less unpleasant than those ordained for the fish. Indeed, the fishing analogy breaks down at this point, since the outcome of the good reading experience is pleasure, not pain; and even in your farthest-fetched imaginings you don't end up on someone's dinner plate. And what I gained from E. Nesbit, even at that ludicrously grown-up age, was the strongest possible charge of elation and well-being. Here was an author who understood to the full what pleased child readers, while not eschewing a tongue-in-cheek, adult detachment from the business in hand. Her books hadn't ruled themselves out for an adult readership, even if the fullest enraptured assent was confined to the eight-year-old, who needed no awareness of breakthrough narrative strategies to enjoy their unprecedented effects.

By keeping one foot, or half a foot, in an adult camp, as it were, E.Nesbit took out an insurance policy against the kind of mild derision that attaches itself to a lot of past children's authors. She wasn't at all like her contemporary Angela Brazil (for instance), who by her unrestrained assumption of schoolgirlishness – 'I say! What a jinky joke!' – set herself up as a target for mockers and parodists of the future. Every children's-books commentator has had a field day with Brazil's baloney – you can't resist it – yet, as I've said, she broke away in her own fashion from the glooms of the past, and ensured a heyday for a special brand of schoolgirl exuberance. It's just that, for enduring charm, subtlety and readability on the author's terms, you have to look to E. Nesbit (the Nesbit of the Bastable stories, that is, the Psammead duo, *The House of Arden* and one or two others; not *The Railway Children* or a lot of retold tales) – to Nesbit, and her great idiosyncratic predecessor Lewis Carroll; and, some way behind these two but nonetheless continuing to hold her own, Richmal Crompton and William.

I loved *Alice* but not for its narrative impetus; its commonsense absurdities and whirlwind logic were the qualities that counted, in Carroll's back-to-front universe. A breathtaking inventiveness made *Alice* a joy to read. But it didn't keep you awake half the night, frantically turning the pages while clutching a torch smuggled under the bedclothes, agog to discover *what happens next*. That's the prerogative of a different type of fiction, 'modern', if you like, in the sense of being fully attuned to the spirit of the present, specially directed at readers of the mid-century, my generation. It can include survivals from the previous generation's top titles too.

By the time I got around to Nesbit, late on, I was aware of certain patterns, strands and spheres of influence marking the whole field of children's literature. Richmal Crompton (say) owes something – a tone, no more, a wry effect – to Nesbit, who owes something to Lewis Carroll. And so on. And as new departures and attitudes peculiar to the age get widely disseminated, you find bread-and-butter storytellers – hordes of them – massing behind the clued-up innovators. Angela Brazil, as I say, was an innovator, for all her preposterousness, with literary effects both engaging and egregious. Although we made fun of her, even as children, she came closer to meeting our requirements, if only we'd realised it, than all those earlier, hopeless authors working within the domain of dismal scenarios featuring emotional upheavals at primitive boarding schools, or creators of obtuse Victorian fathers who couldn't tell their daughters from a daisy chain. Dead as doornails, the lot of them, we thought, with their eyes turned heavenwards and their unpalatable palpitations.

Among the bread-and-butter brigade, though perhaps with a lighter touch than many, was Mrs George de Horne Vaizey, born in 1860, Edith Nesbit's junior by two years. In 1972 or '73 I was living in Blackheath, in south-east London, and already far gone in obsessive children's-books accumulation. One of my haunts was a small antique market held every Saturday at the Standard near the Old Dover Road. Here I replaced my Penguin E. Nesbits, old reading copies, with five or six T. Fisher Unwin first editions, red binding, gilt lettering and cover illustrations, and H.R.Millar's Norfolk-suited boys and tam-o'shantered girls taking amulets and phoenixes and singular carpets in their stride. These were well-read copies, battered but still wonderfully solid and desirable, and it added something to their attractiveness that I was buying them from a market stall not far from the spot where adventures had befallen some prominent Nesbit characters. The Bastables, for example, were well acquainted with Blackheath village, Vanburgh Castle, All Saints church and the nearby yacht pond. It was on the Heath that the intrepid small family lurked in ambush to waylay an unwary traveller and restore the fortunes of the ancient House of Bastable. It was here they learnt a lesson from old Lord Tottenham when their behaviour verged on the dishonourable.

Blackheath and Lewisham, Croom's Hill, Greenwich Park, the pond.... as if all that wasn't enough, the Nesbit books from the market at the Standard had an interesting inscription displayed on their flyleaves. Christine Olive de Horne Vaizey, from Mummy. Mummy was Mrs George de H.V., and young Christine Olive would have been suitably aged to make the most of the Bastable and Psammead stories as they were issued by their publisher. So the books I held in my hand were association copies, in a way. In another way, they had unexpected associations for myself. Suddenly I was back in Belfast, and up the stairs to the juvenile section of a library I hastened. It wasn't the Donegall Road but the Falls Road branch, to which I was returning a book I had borrowed but hadn't warmed to. *Pixie O'Shaughnessy*, it was called, and the author was a Mrs George de Horne Vaizey. Misled by the 'Irishness' of the title, I had taken the book out hoping it might reflect a modicum of what I considered common sense about the Irish (this didn't preclude fantasy or adventure, indeed, but it *did* preclude 'shure' and 'begorrah' and 'Oi like a relish to my tay'). But *Pixie O'Shaughnessy*, alas, hadn't risen above the notion of Ireland as a country populated solely by flamboyant families living in merry disorder in falling-down castles. Poor or not – and they always *are* poor – these families never lack the wherewithal to dispatch their daughters to English boarding schools where the Irish girls' madcap qualities attract attention. With the full measure of a ten-year-old's capacity for indignation, I resented the slur on the whole country signalled by the antics and the brogue. I knew the term 'stage Irish' and had already been primed to deplore the lazy tendency of authors to gain an effect by thickening Irish speech and distorting our vowel sounds.

It wasn't only the factitious idiom that got my goat. *Pixie* and similar stories had an awfully antiquated air as well: or so it seemed to me at the time. It made a difference when the poverty, picturesque shambles and ritualised belligerence of the storybook Irish were tempered by a modern tone. For example, these qualities, and others, featured in a book I liked enormously, *The Mad O'Haras* by Patricia Lynch, whose buoyancy and bravado put it in a contemporary category – though you would have to say it's not so much modern as timeless. (It was published in 1948.) It does indeed contain a tumbledown castle and a family feud, but these work well within the overall scheme of things coming out right in the end. Other Patricia Lynch books were equally charming and inspiriting, within the range of whatever age-group they were aimed at. Perhaps because she was herself Irish, this author made a merry medley of her turf-cutters' donkeys and tinkers and ballad-sellers and apple-women and endearing grey geese, and never sounded a patronising note for an opinionated young reader to take exception to. Many of her books were there on a shelf of the Falls Road Library when I visited it for the first time in 1953 or '54, along with much else, patriotically orientated as befitted the locality, or – Blyton, Biggles, Breary, Bunter – pandering for all it was worth to the populist requirements of its clientele.

3. READING BY THE FIRE

Come back, all ye enthusiasms of yesteryear
Into a retrospective ode's proclaimed rhapsodics ...
Douglas Dunn, 'Libraries: A Celebration'

THE NOVELIST BRIAN MOORE, growing up in Clifton Street in the 1920s and '30s in a family of nine children, was sometimes sent on a cultural errand. His father, Dr Moore, enjoyed certain privileges through being a person of note in Catholic circles in Belfast, and among them was the right to have first choice of new books coming into the Falls Road Library where his friend Joe Fitzsimmons was head librarian. Not that busy Dr Moore was often able to visit the library in person. It was more likely that Brian, or one of the other young Moores, would be given the task of collecting the new library books and carrying them home in a suitcase.

It was quite a hazardous trek, all the way from Clifton Street to the Falls, for a middle-class schoolboy in the 1930s wearing short grey flannel trousers and a St Malachy's School blazer. The route would have taken him along Carrick Hill, into Millfield, Divis Street and then up the main thoroughfare with its teeming side-streets containing raggedy children all endowed with Falls Road jeering skills. It was worth enduring the catcalls and threatened fisticuffs, however. The

Moore children benefited from their father's standing in the broader district, being given the run of the juvenile section of the library before the local hordes of grubby borrowers were allowed to swarm in for their weekly dose of *Just William* or *Milly-Molly-Mandy*.

No doubt the Moores made the most of their special position. I don't know which titles Brian would have coveted, though. In later life, he claimed to remember nothing of his early reading between the weekly story papers the *Magnet* and *Gem*, and James Joyce's *Ulysses*. Probably authors such as Hemingway or Kafka would have filled the gap, for he certainly read something. And he had opinions. From about the age of fourteen on, he took a poor view of his father's taste in literature. Between Ngaio Marsh and Maurice Walsh, the library books of Dr Moore were a slight embarrassment to his would-be highbrow son. Brian once declared with a kind of good-humoured derision that his father had considered Kate O'Brien to be a great novelist. Well!

Kate O'Brien is not greatly to my taste either, and certainly wouldn't have been in the past, when I haunted the Falls Road Library in search of mysteries and sensations. Picture a darkening winter's afternoon in the early 1950s, snow descending from heavily laden clouds above the Black Mountain, adding a new layer to already thickly coated pavements and filling in the footprints of shoppers and stragglers, old women wrapped in shawls cursing the unaccustomed weather and children revelling in it. Soon the whole thing will turn to slush and drabness, but just for the moment it is pristine and prodigious. And I envisage myself in the middle of it, wearing a navy nap coat over a skirt and jumper, and thick woollen socks stuffed into Wellington boots, heading for the library and something wonderfully seasonal to chime with the atmosphere outside.

What I'm returning is *The Secret of Red Gate Farm*, perhaps, featuring never-failing Nancy Drew (' "I'm proud of you, Nancy", her father declared earnestly, "... on account of the way you rounded up that gang of counterfeiters" '); or one of the Brockhampton Press's Brock Books with the jaunty Scottie dog logo. Once inside, I scan the shelves in search of – what? How am I going to decide between *The Secret of the Lodge* and *The Secret of the Shuttered Lodge*? Between *Merry Marches On* and *Mumfie Marches On*? *The Intrusion of Peggy* and *The Intrusion of Nicola*? How can I possibly choose Freda M. Hurt over Freda C. Bond? I expect I will stick to an author I know. Once the children's librarian has stamped it, I see myself carrying off something like *Strangers at Snowfell*, the third 'Jillies' book by Malcolm Saville which opens on a snowbound train in Westmoreland, from which five children are precipitated by their author towards an isolated farmhouse and an imprisoned scientist in need of rescue by intrepid juveniles. Or it might be Elinor Lyon's *We Daren't Go A-Hunting*, in which it's necessary for the Highland brother-and-sister team of Ian and Sovra Kennedy to don a lot of extra jerseys before leaving the house to scupper a crew of stag hunters. ('What's it like out yonder?' 'Starting to blizz again.') Or – still in Scotland – *Alison's Christmas Adventure* by Sheila Stuart, with the laurels in the garden covered in a thick crust of white and a lot of strangers up to no good ('Is the Professor's interest in geology genuine?' Well, actually, no it isn't.) Or perhaps I would simply opt for the most generic title of all, *Snowed Up with a Secret*, by the long-forgotten author Agnes Miall, and entrench myself in its wintry chicanery complete with jewel thief and near-fatal misjudgement on the part of its young protagonists. Their tremendous pluck is never in question, though. 'It had been a nerve-racking trip, creeping out of the silent house and through the garden to discover what had happened at the bottom of the drain-pipe.' I bet.

If it's snow I'm after, I might do worse than pluck a Bessie Marchant title off the shelf (I'm sure they were there). But these girls' adventures in exotic places like Russia and British Columbia lacked a necessary ingredient, a flavour of modern times. Anything conspicuously out of date, without humour to enliven it, or quaintness to prettify it, gave me the pip. It's only as a collector, well on in life, that I've come to relish this ancient author, known in her day as 'the girl's Henty'. (I couldn't read Henty either.) I now have a good selection of Marchants on my own bookshelves, all in splendid bindings. *A Dangerous Mission* of 1918, for example, sports a cover image of a pine forest starkly outlined against Russian snows, and an inadequately but picturesquely dressed girl bravely grappling with both. Dark blue, black and a greyish white are the colours. *Hope's Tryst* (1905), another northern tale, shows a bearded Russian speeding merrily along in a troika in muted shades of blue, green, white and orange, for this one is set in 'bare, grey Kiakhta, which stands on the borderland between Siberia and Mongolia'. It is, indeed, an incongruous setting for the eponymous Hope, who is pinpointed straight away as 'a winsome picture of English girlhood'. Hope, true to form, is also endowed with a full measure of English spunk and uprightness, attributes alien to most of the foreigners around her. *A Countess from Canada* (1911) – whose title is explained only in the closing pages – likewise illumines the backwoods of Keewatin country with her moral worth. In or about 1953, she and all her ilk would certainly have got up my piety-resistant nose.

Bessie Marchant, L.T. Meade. I have already stated my aversion to Meade (no one in their right mind could possibly enjoy her books for girls). But, if the content is one thing, the bindings are another. They are irresistible to the collector who is driven, as Elizabeth Bowen said on the subject of dress, 'by the exactions of her particular whim'. So: I confess to owning a handful of Meades including *The Hill-Top Girl* with its striking art nouveau silhouetted figure on the cover, and *The Manor School* which comes in boards depicting a pair of enchanting Edwardian schoolgirls in front of a spooky-looking mansion, all done in shades of dark red, cream, black and gold. ... Sometimes, from incorrigible light-mindedness, I find myself composing nonsense jingles in the middle of the night. They include such things as clerihews and nursery rhyme parodies. One of the latter was sparked off by L.T. Meade, plus the inevitability of the collecting impulse getting out of hand:

Mary, Mary, isn't it scary,
How your shelves do grow!
With *Silver Snaffles* and *Bunkle Baffles* ...
And pretty Meades all in a row.

Silver Snaffles by Primrose Cumming is of course a pony book – another genre I never really took to (though I read some specimens of it along with everything else). Thinking about the great 1950s' vogue for stories featuring girls in britches besotted with horses, brought on another nighttime parody:

I had a little pony book,
Its name was *Chestnut Gold*.
I lent it to a baby,
He was red-faced and bold!
He snatched it, he scratched it,
He dragged it through the mire.
I'll never lend my book again,
To face that baby's ire.

(Clearly this baby is a version of myself in damaging mode.)
The wonderful thing about the libraries of the mid-century was the range of their accumulated stock-in-trade. Whatever tickled your fancy – time travel, the restoration

of family fortunes or eventful English girls' boarding-school life – it would be there on the shelf waiting to enthral you.

The Falls Road repository of this abundance is, like its counterpart on the Donegall Road, a creation of the Belfast architectural firm of Watt and Tulloch, and likewise bestows a touch of attractiveness and dignity on a raucous neighbourhood. Also in common with the Donegall Road, its children's section is housed at the top of an imposing staircase, and contains enough specimens of anglocentric adventuring to undermine any young local reader's instinctive anglophobia. Or so you might think. In practice, it didn't work quite like that. We Falls Road eleven-year-olds lapped up the doings of a range of characters from William Brown to Captain W.E. Johns's Worrals, all of them as English as George Stubbs's Haymakers, and – with the Second World War not too far in the past – as patriotic as Captain Mainwaring of Walmington-on-Sea. Their priorities were unreservedly ours, for the duration of the story. The characters we read about were simply enhanced versions of ourselves, with nothing to be resented or despised about them. We experienced no psychological resistance to an English ethos, as purveyed by our dearest authors. Once out of the reading trance, though, we reserved the right to revert to a statutory verbal defiance of England and English ways, with the fullest consciousness of wrongs inflicted on Clowney Street, Derby Street and all the other Falls Road streets. Belligerence was the mode in which it was suitable to entertain the idea of England, yet at the same time, England was the source of all our book-induced elation. At ten or eleven, though, we remained happily unaware of any paradoxical element contained in this situation.

The historian Paul Larmour describes the Falls Road Library's architectural style as English-Edwardian 'Wrenaissance', mentioning in particular 'the good scrolling art nouveau ironwork to the stairway inside'. Local artist and sculptor Rosamond Praeger contributed to the decorative effect of the whole building with her splendid spandrel figures of Art, Literature and Science (still in place as I write, more than a century later). At nine or ten, I'd have been in such a hurry to get into the building and reach the bookshelves that I probably wouldn't consciously have registered such shining details – but I believe they worked their priceless effect none the less. I *was* familiar with the marble statue known as 'The Fairy Fountain', also by Rosamond Praeger; and when I was very small it was this I'd make a beeline for, whenever some adult (mother, grandmother) brought me on a special visit to the Ulster Museum in the Stranmillis Road. The sleeping child at the fountain, holding her water jug in a drooping hand and unaware of the scrutiny of two elves emerging tentatively to peer at her, spoke strongly to a five-year-old's sense of homely and indigenous magic. It was redolent, too, of a nursery beauty. W.B. Yeats's 'The Stolen Child' came later, and had something of the same power to suggest the opposing allurements of the world and the otherworld:

Away with us he's going,
The solemn-eyed.
He'll hear no more the lowing
Of the calves on the warm hillside.
Or the kettle on the hob,
Sing peace into his breast,
Or see the brown mice bob,
Round and round the oatmeal-chest.

Whatever books I'd borrowed from the Falls Road Library on that archetypal afternoon in mid-winter, I would carry them across the road to the nearest bus stop and join the queue for an Andersonstown or Glen Road trolley-bus, either of which would deposit me safely at the corner of St James's Park, only a couple of hundred yards from my own back gate. By now, the street-lamps would be lit and casting eerie shadows on the thickening snow – snow all the more sparkling for its inevitable impermanence (like the capacity to read childish adventure stories with uncritical abandon). I'd make my way down the Park, tramping along with my Wellingtons producing a satisfying crunch at every step, turning right into St James's Avenue and beginning to hurry when I see our lighted kitchen window at the end of the Avenue beckoning me on. Even in my over-active imagination I can't think I'm liable to perish in the blizzard like Lucy Gray since every inch of this territory, in every kind of weather, is as familiar to me as the pages of the *Rainbow Annual* for 1945. ... And soon I'm indoors, getting thawed by a blazing fire, cheerful adults about the place and a tea consisting of home-made wheaten bread, a piece of cake and a beaker of milk before me. And reading, reading, reading.

The Falls Road in all its variety from the cobblestones of the Pound Loney to the big houses of Fruithill Park impinged on my consciousness early on. But it wasn't until I'd become a pupil at St Dominic's Girls' Grammar School in 1954 that I really got to grips with its side streets, its public buildings like the Royal Victoria Hospital and the Swimming Baths, its chip shops and dingy cafés and forbidden flea-ridden picture houses such as the Clonard or the Diamond (the Broadway Cinema near our house, with its trees in tubs at each side of the entrance and its uniformed commissionaires, was a much superior establishment). Many of these places I never set foot in, but I hold in my head a mental image of each. Dunville Park, St Comgall's School, Ross's, Greeve's, Blackstaff Mill .... Just beyond St Dominic's School was St Paul's Church – which again I had no reason to enter, my parish church being St John's farther up the road – Cavendish Street, Cavendish Square (built in 1892 and named after Lord Frederick Cavendish, the Chief Secretary of Ireland, murdered in Dublin's Phoenix Park ten years previously); Springfield Road, McQuillan Street, Theresa Street, Waterford Street, Linden Street, Clonard Street, Dunlewy Street ... all the streets and streets of red-brick rows, all housing a community of the self-taught, if taught at all. And autodidacts among them had the library itself, right there on the corner of Sevastapol Street and facing the main road, to further their educational ambitions. For which credit is due to Dr Andrew Carnegie (Bravo! again). And Bravo, Dr Moore (for his support of the library)! And the early child borrowers before the First World War who ensured the juvenile section was kept well supplied with classics and picture books!

(Belfast autodidacts of the past were predominantly left-wing in politics and washed their hands of Orange and Green, Protestant and Catholic. If penniless, which they usually were, they were also very resourceful. One of them, I was told, was so devoted to literature that he undertook the feat of transcribing by hand the whole of James Joyce's *A Portrait of the Artist as a Young Man*. He tracked down a copy to a local library [the Falls or the Donegall Road, I am not sure which], borrowed it and kept renewing it, and sat down with his notebook and pen until the undertaking was complete. He then had a copy of the book in his possession. One can only stand speechless in the face of such tenacity and exertion.)

Imagine getting locked inside a library when the lights had been switched off, everyone else had gone home, and the book-aroma, muted when other borrowers were about the place, had suddenly become overwhelming! Would this be scary or thrilling? Would you begin to panic, casting aside whatever had kept you so engrossed that you'd overlooked the signs of everyone leaving, banging on the door and calling to be let out – or would you, on the other hand, decide to make the most of the unexpected freedom to wander through an endless succession of adventures and fantasies, unchecked by everyday constraints? Would you relish the solitude inside the library, its myriad possibilities? Or fear you might merge with the books altogether, and become just a watered-down version of Anne of Green Gables, or Kate Crackernuts? As darkness fell, would your imagination run away with you, enabling Abner Brown or – more locally – the ghost of Old Corby from Sandy Row,[1] to take on a palpable existence? In the library at night, says Alberto Manguel, 'the atmosphere changes. Sounds become muffled, thoughts grow louder.'[2] And where would those thoughts lead you – into an M.R. James diabolical mezzotint scenario, or towards a cupboard in a dark corner where lurked the children's bogey, Rawhead and Bloody-bones? Not likely: I expect common sense would suggest the prospect of rescue wasn't too far away, and that, in the meantime, the reading opportunity should be embraced (as long as the reading material was suitably unthreatening).

It couldn't have happened, of course, not in a well-regulated city library like the Falls or the Donegall Road, with inflexible opening and closing times, eagle-eyed employees and no scope for any juvenile addict to fall,

---

[1] *Haunted Belfast* by Joe Baker (2007) includes the story of Old Corby and many other local ghost stories.
[2] *The Library at Night* (2006).

unnoticed, into a reading reverie. For two young girls in Elizabeth Enright's *Thimble Summer*, it was a different story. *Their* local library is 'an old-fashioned frame building set back from the road among thick-foliaged maple trees'. We're in a small Wisconsin town called Blaiseville, during a hot 1930s' summer, and the two friends, Garnet and Citronella, have settled themselves on a broad window seat in the library to engage in a session of reading. One has her nose embedded in Kipling's *The Jungle Book*, while the other enjoys a piece of flimflam called *Duchess Olga*. They read on and on ... until the realisation dawns that the librarian has gone and left them and the place is locked up. 'Slowly the dusk sifted into the room. The bookcases looked tall and solemn.... There was no telephone in the library and no electric light.' They start to feel 'as if all those books were alive and listening' – and that the books' intentions are perhaps not altogether benign.

But all ends well, though it's nearly midnight before a search party locates the missing readers and restores them to the bosom of their families. 'Yes sir!' exclaims their principal rescuer. 'Don't you be fooled! Those ain't two little girls you see settin' up there; those are two genuwine bookworms, couldn't stop reading long enough to come home. Planning to take up permanent residence in the liberry from now on, ain'tcha?'

For some of us local Belfast bookworms, taking up permanent residence in a library – if not an actual library, then a figurative one – was a measure of the way our lives would unfold.

'On his way home he called in the Falls Road Library for a book of Irish History for Alec and it was nearly five o'clock when he arrived home.' Young Colm MacNeill from the Beechmount area of west Belfast in Michael McLaverty's novel *Call My Brother Back* (1939), takes the library for granted like everyone else in the district in 1920 or thereabouts. It seems a permanent fixture of the neighbourhood. But soon it is going to have an inappropriate function imposed on it. This is the disaffected Falls, and trouble is brewing (trouble is always brewing). In 1923 the library is occupied by B-Specials with their sandbags, rifles and armoured trucks, their distrust of the nationalist population and scant regard for books.

I don't know how long the requisitioning of the library continues, or what the effect on neighbourhood readers is. But gradually a shaky peace returns to the Falls and normal life, including book-borrowing, is resumed. Before this happens, McLaverty's Colm MacNeill on his way to school has had to dodge bullets in the side streets as snipers of both factions shoot at anything that moves. 'He saw a man in his shirt sleeves firing a revolver towards the Protestant quarters.' (I was seventeen or so when I first read this novel, and even then I felt it had something of the quality of a children's classic, with its lucid descriptive virtuosity and vernacular aplomb. And in particular, I loved the three young brothers' summer excursion up the Black Mountain, with the heat striking up in thick waves from the stony path, the heathery summit and the view of Belfast spread out in the hollow below. Looking at all the church spires, wouldn't you think, laughs brother Alec, 'that it was a Christian town?' Well, wouldn't you?) With the shooting and uproar in the side streets of the Falls, young Colm is getting a foretaste of what will occur again and again – and later in the century, with the utmost savagery and destruction. But for me, growing up at a time of relative adjustment to the status quo, the old Falls dissension, loyalties and clandestine confederacies are tinged with a rebel glamour and integrity.

I never saw a mob get out of hand, or witnessed violence inflicted and reciprocated. No riots broke out in St James's Avenue or nearby La Salle Park.[3] A seemly and uncontentious atmosphere prevailed, and, if I was drawn to danger and disruption, it was only in my head (or in some of the books I read). The history of Northern Ireland had made it clear to me that all the right was on the side of the nationalist minority, and I indulged, along with many other people, in the statutory condemnation of Unionism and Orangeism, asserted my Irish identity,[4] and got on with school, home life

---

[3] This had changed by 1971, when, from my parents' bedroom window, I watched a riot erupt on a patch of waste ground a hundred yards away on the Donegall Road, following the introduction of internment.

[4] Half Irish-Catholic and half Ulster-Protestant, though the former was a lot shakier than I realised at the time: see my book, *A Twisted Root* (2012).

and copious reading. If I'd been aware of it at the time, I might have gone along with Benedict Kiely's[5] view that Belfast had somehow been brought to a better frame of mind. The old riotous instincts were subdued, he believed, in the aftermath of the recent war, and not before time – for no inhabitants of the city 'could congratulate themselves on the uncouth, vicious thing that comes to life at intervals to burn and kill and destroy'. His optimism was not well-founded, but 1950s' gloss and opportunism had produced a deceptive calm, even while ineradicable alienation was simmering underneath.

Past eruptions of violence – riots and ructions – could only be viewed with dismay, by those in possession of their sober senses. However, it is possible to allow the emphasis to fall differently, to take street fighting out of the realm of reality, for instance, by imposing a sportive overtone on top of it, as F. Frankfort Moore does in his book of 1914 *The Truth about Ulster* (see p. 134 below); or dignifying it by association, as we find in the comment of the Edwardian essayist Robert Lynd. 'Belfast, when maddened,' he writes, 'is as capable of a Papist hunt, as the French revolutionaries were of a hunt for aristocrats. I have a friend, indeed,' he goes on, 'who, whenever he had been out looking on during a Belfast riot, used to go home and read Carlyle's *French Revolution*. He said that in movement and colour it read like a description of things in Belfast.'[6] And, 'rioting was

---

[5] *Counties of Contention* (1945).
[6] Robert Lynd, *The Orange Tree* (1926).

the popular pastime', agrees the painter Paul Henry,[7] born in 1877 in University Road, observing the heaps of paving stones piled up for ammunition in every disturbed locality he ventures into. 'Regular rioting', too, enlivened the 1920s' childhood of Paddy Devlin[8] in crummy Conway Street between the Falls Road and the Shankill. The Devlin house had once been occupied by a gunman and sported walls pockmarked with bullet holes to prove it. Between rioting and Orange drums coming up the Grosvenor Road with their boom-boom intimations of menace, the infant Paddy Devlin was occasionally scared out of his wits and forced to dive for refuge under the bed.

Brian Moore as a schoolboy, on the other hand, positively relished the thrill of watching thousands of Orangemen assemble and parade under his bedroom window, in full understanding, as he put it, 'that you and yours are the very enemy they seek to destroy'.[9] The Moores who in the 1930s lived in Clifton Street opposite the headquarters of the Orange Order, were the only Catholic family in Belfast to have a grandstand view of these proceedings, and Brian made the most of this accident of habitation. He could look, but he wasn't allowed out, of course, unlike the Divis Street boys of an earlier generation, recalled by the journalist T.J. Campbell,[10] who regularly engaged in

[7] Paul Henry, *Further Reminiscences* (1978).

[8] Paddy Devlin, *Straight Left* (1993).

[9] Brian Moore, 'Bloody Ulster'. *Atlantic Monthly* (September 1970).

[10] T.J. Campbell, *Fifty Years of Ulster 1890-1940* (1941).

an exchange of missiles with their counterparts from a Ragged School on the Shankill, around the Twelfth of July.

Brian Moore emerged into the world in August 1921, just as a volley of rifle shots rang out in Clifton Street outside his mother's bedroom window, causing her to think a bomb had exploded. It's a particularly inflammable period in Belfast's history. We're still in the early 1920s when the future poet and novelist George Buchanan from Kilwaughter near Larne, aged seventeen-and-a-half, starts work at the *Northern Whig* office near the Docks, and needs a special permit to cross the city after the night shift on the News Desk. 'I am obliged to walk nervously to my distant digs through a city under curfew,' he recalls.[11] The night-time walk features burning buildings and flying bullets, and by the time he has made it back to his lodgings on the Cliftonville Road, the young reporter is in such a state of nerves that he envisages himself as a bullet-ridden corpse in the street; or, if he has got as far as his front door in one piece, imagines a gunman waiting to pounce on him, hidden 'perhaps behind the gable or inside the hall ...' . These are recurring images of fear and horror fostered by Belfast in any one of its unruly phases.

Though the noise of shooting and shouting in the streets was inescapable, if you happened to be born and grow up in Belfast at a particular time, there were those who managed to evade the worst of the commotions issuing from the

[11] George Buchanan, *Green Seacoast* (1959).

slums. The naturalist Edward Allworthy Armstrong,[12] for example, up the Cave Hill with his binoculars on the trail of merlins and curlews, scarcely registers the clatter of machine-gun fire down below. Even the news of 2,000 armed Sinn Feiners 'drilling over the mountain' is brushed aside by the imperturbable investigator of natural, as opposed to revolutionary, history. Birdsong means more to him than any party song.

Or take Denis Ireland, lolling about at a suburban tennis club in 1921 or thereabouts, and comparing the distant popping of guns to the ping of tennis balls bouncing off racquets in the hands of immaculately clad, sporty young people like something out of Michael Arlen. 'The poppings begin again,' he writes. ... 'Well, who cares? Deuce, vantage ... if people like to murder one another in the streets of Belfast, let them – it has nothing to do with us.' Actually, it would be wrong to quote that remark of Denis Ireland's[13] without making it clear that he's reproducing an atmosphere, not expressing an opinion. A middle-class hauteur in relation to the rough-and-tumble of the slums is something he's familiar with, having grown up in serene Malone, but doesn't necessarily share. He's a social observer and raconteur whose reminiscences are cast in the form of evocative jottings; the tone is faintly sardonic and mischievous and always dispassionate. He is playacting, for

---

[12] Edward Allworthy Armstrong, *Birds of the Grey Wind* (1940).
[13] Denis Ireland, *From the Irish Shore* (1936).

instance, when he shudders dramatically at the thought of the Black Mountain and the Falls Road, lethal territory 'from which there sometimes came the sound of shots': a world away from the tranquil suburbs of his upbringing. 'Down in the darkness of the garden there was peace, a single ash tree standing sentinel between the tennis lawn and the lush meadows of the Lagan Valley.' But even Denis Ireland cannot go about his business in the city without coming face-to-face with reminders of rioting, in the form of smashed windows and knots of policemen with rifles stationed at every incendiary street corner.

Different eras, and different social classes, affected styles of upbringing and subsequent recollections of blandness or discord. Take James O. Hannay (better known as George A. Birmingham), for instance. Born in 1865 in the middle of a sedate terrace opposite Queen's University, this clergyman's son suffered no agitation, as far as we know, on account of encroaching mobs bent on badness, or violence erupting within sight or sound of his father's house. Sandy Row, where trouble broke out in 1872, wasn't too far away. But street-trouble never extended beyond the line cutting off the righteous from the riotous. Within the Hannay household, all was calm and decorous. The autobiography, *Pleasant Places*, which George A. Birmingham wrote in 1934, evokes a singularly agreeable Ulster childhood. When you come down to it, however, the author finds little to commend about Belfast itself, apart from the spirit of protestantism – with a small 'p' – which animates its inhabitants. (Sectarian lunacy, which he observed with a kind of sardonic detachment, inspired his *tour de force* of 1912, *The Red Hand of Ulster*, with its jovial appraisal of the anti-Home Rule brouhaha and all its twists and turns.)

The happy childhood and boyhood to which Birmingham pays tribute in *Pleasant Places* is derived from family circumstances, siblings and cousins and jolly seasonal activities: 'In summer we picnicked at Crawfurdsburn, bathed at Clandeboye and built ourselves forts high up among the branches of trees. In winter we gathered round Christmas trees, played riotously at Blind Man's Buff and, fearfully, snapped burning raisins from the dish in front of an awful dragon ...'. As he grew older, there were holidays on the north coast of Antrim, and a good deal of dancing and tennis-playing took place. It adds up to a glimpse into middle-class life in Belfast towards the end of the nineteenth century, which turns out to be less stodgy than we had imagined, more akin to an E. Nesbit sort of blitheness.

George A. Birmingham was the son of a clergyman, as I've said, and a clergyman himself; and when he refers to one of only two public monuments in Belfast at the time as 'a black statue to the memory of a Presbyterian divine called Dr Cook [*sic*]', misspelling his name as 'Cook' without an 'e', you have to wonder if he's affecting a Church of Ireland disdain for lesser, non-establishment systems of religion such as Presbyterianism. He must have known the correct spelling perfectly well, as Dr Cooke, with his riproaring ministry at May Street Presbyterian church, was among the most prominent Belfast figures of the nineteenth century. Or Birmingham may have been referring obliquely to the fact that Dr Cooke started life in Maghera as Henry Macook, without the 'e', to take him down a peg or two.

This Belfast, or Northern Irish, scorn for different religions filters all the way down the social scale, and it wasn't (as we see) confined to Protestantism and Catholicism. John Morrow, writing in the 1990s,[14] recalls the arrival of his grandparents in Belfast in the early part of the twentieth century. They came with their possessions on a horse-drawn cart, and instantly received in their faces such an acrid blast of grime and soot that they nearly shot right back to the countryside they had lately abandoned. They stuck it out, however, despite 'the gasworks [which] scringed and wailed the night long, at times giving out a powerful stench, as if of one accord a million tom cats were pissing painfully on hot cinders'. In the daytime a different stench, reminiscent of burning bones, emanated from the mudflats of the River Lagan at low tide. But these and other annoyances of the back streets off the lower Ormeau Road, such as overcrowded living conditions, were as nothing, as far as Morrow's robust Episcopalian grandmother was concerned, compared to the proximity of Presbyterians. Presbyterians, whom she called Blackmouths (a term of abuse dating back to the seventeenth century), were, it's true, to be

---

[14] John Morrow, *Pruck: A Life in Bits and Pieces* (1999).

abominated to a lesser degree than Roman Catholics; but in the areas of theological error and social inferiority, there wasn't much to choose between the two.

Marcus Crouch's study of children's reading between 1900 and 1960 has a felicitous title. It is called *Treasure Seekers and Borrowers*.[15] The phrase is derived from books by E. Nesbit and Mary Norton; and, taken in isolation, what it signifies for some of us is the start of a lifetime's intimacy with libraries and the riches therein. That's the premier activity we threw ourselves into, as children, browsing for book treasures and acquiring them on loan. In the special case of Belfast libraries, too, as an added godsend, you found – and find – no demarcation of books along sectarian lines. Protestant or Catholic, it made no odds, as far as reading choices went. Worlds beyond the local sectarian rift were available to all; and for us readers, library frequenters, even Katy Carr – even, God help us, Eyeore the Donkey – might work at some level against inherited bigotries. At the very least, whatever convictions we nourished, we'd have learnt, over time, not to be too dismissive of different sets of convictions held by others. I am not saying that readers, in any circumstances, are incapable of turning into rioters. But I do believe that knowledge obtained from books, leading to informed historical and social awareness, is bound to have a moderating effect on atavistic aggressions.

---

[15] The Library Association (1962).

So: as treasure seekers and borrowers, we were getting a good grounding in the ways of chivalry, uprightness and fair play, courtesy of public school authors such as John Finnemore with his 'Teddy Lester' series. Time after time, we rejoiced in the downfall of bad prefects and fourth-form sneaks, applauded the capture of crooks by bands of resourceful schoolchildren, and cheered on the wartime spy-catchers whose quarries were sometimes literally sat upon. I'm talking about myself and my friends, and also about library aficionados all over Belfast, all of whose behaviour must have been affected by what they ingested. The minds of non-readers, 'outdoor' children, those deficient in literacy or concentration, or just relentlessly unimaginative, are a closed book to us. And here's a tiny paradox: the stories we cherished contained few readers. True, in the pages of adventure stories, too much is going on for anyone to sit down and devote themselves to a book; but the frequent implication is that they wouldn't bother to do so anyway. 'Do you like reading?' When this question is put to a young kidnapped Count by one of his kinder captors who has brought along a book to cheer him up (in Violet Needhams's 1957 offering, *The Red Rose of Ruvina*), back comes the answer, 'Not much.' And Agnes M. Miall's Perry, in *The Vanishing Trick* (1951), is described as 'the eldest of the trio [of juvenile adventurers] and the only one who went in much for reading ...'. Reading, when it's mentioned at all, is presented as a rather eccentric occupation. For us in the real world, though, it is not only normal, but essential. It's filling gaps, inundating us with excitements lacking in our everyday lives; and much else besides.

One young treasure seeker and borrower, with whom my visits to the Falls library might just have overlapped, is the future poet and Belfast laureate Ciaran Carson, born in Raglan Street, educated at St Mary's Christian Brothers School, and (for a time at least) a Falls Road Library habitué. 'I'd walk on down Clonard Street on my way home from school,' he writes, 'turn down Odessa Street and Sevastopol Street, to emerge at the impressive sandstone façade of the Falls Road branch of the Andrew Carnegie library'. The rage for reading soon drove him farther afield, however – as it did myself – into the dodgy unfamiliarity of the Protestant Shankill, for example, with its library on the corner of Mountjoy Street, which he used to frequent 'in search of Biggles books because I had exhausted the entire Biggles stock of the Falls Library'.

The Shankill Road branch was built between 1926 and 1928 to a design by T.W. Henry (architect brother of the painter Paul Henry). Paul Larmour admires the restraint of its conception – 'just a little curved Doric portico to add dignity to a public building'. Like most attractive small libraries, it is sturdy and shapely in appearance. I went there too for a time, but I found it too out-of-way, and with no obvious advantages over places more conveniently sited. Like Ciaran Carson, though, I was driven to try out every possible source of reading material in the city, before settling on those most suitable for my purposes. The Donegall Road branch was another venue that drew him towards it, like Desperate Dan on the trail of a cow pie, even though it also lay outside the zone of safety on the sectarian map of Belfast. (This was true for me as well, but since the library was situated just at the far end of my own road, it didn't seem to make any odds.) Coming face-to-face with its palpable calm, Ciaran Carson says, 'one became aware of the democracy of print, whose ink still lingered in the date-stamp redolence of pine shelves and brown linoleum'. He goes on: 'After acquiring a cache of "Biggles", I liked to wander through the high dark stacks of the Adult section, where dusty sunbeams would illuminate the gold-blocked, arcane numbers of the Dewey Decimal Classification System.'

But what was a young boy in short trousers doing in the Adult section, we might ask? Laying the ground, perhaps, for a future erudition to the nth degree – and an electrifying way of bringing his accumulated knowledge before his readers. In *The Star Factory* of 1997 – his book about Belfast – Carson subjects his native 'dark city' to an extended and inspired reinvention. His approach to Belfast's particulars, its streets and edifices and flotsam and miasmas, is spellbinding and idiosyncratic. Following in the footsteps of Michael McLaverty, forty-odd years later, Carson at one point describes a remembered, or archetypal, walk with his father up the slopes of the Black Mountain. Just before the summit, Carson Senior pauses to light a cigarette, a Park Drive or Woodbine, and makes a downwards gesture with the fag between his fingers, indicating to his son the components of the strung-out city below with its emblems of aggrandisement: biggest shipyard in the world, biggest ropeworks,

> ... the green cupola of the City Hall; the biggest linen mill; Clonard Monastery; Gallaher's tobacco factory; my school; the GPO; and in between, the internecine, regimental terraces of houses and the sprawled, city-wide Armada of tall mill funnels writing diagonals of smoke across the telescopic clarity of our vision. I could see the colour-coded kerbs of Union Jack and Tricolour. I saw my tiny self appearing at the front door of 100 Raglan Street ....

It's a vision of 1950s' Belfast to be looked back on with wonder, conjured up as it is with a masterly eccentricity of orientation. What gives *The Star Factory* its unique flavour is the alternation of foot-off-the-ground narration – not to say a stellar perspective, with the disembodied author hovering over the city like a recording angel – and down-to-earth concern with specifics: the names of businesses in Cornmarket; the rusted bars of the iron railing of the entry at the back of St Gall's Public Elementary School in Waterville Street; the smell of plaster pervading the half-rural housing estates springing up at the farthest, Andersonstown/Suffolk end of the road. Writing in the mid-1990s, Ciaran Carson holds in his head the whole agglomeration, pungency, parochialism, lore, metaphysical route maps and all. ... In the meantime, in the past and under his arm, he has his *Biggles – Secret Agent, Biggles Hits the Trail, Biggles in the Baltic,* in the *Gobi,* in the *South Seas, Biggles* here, there and everywhere, to foster the idea of a highly coloured world with order and method in it, and enlarge his Belfast viewpoint. And, of course, to keep his spirits up.

For Ciaran Carson it was Biggles with his sangfroid that did the trick – 'Whistling softly, he picked up the time-bomb and walked towards the cliff'[16] – and for me it was Bunter. Well, not Billy Bunter himself, indeed, but the vivid world of the Greyfriars School stories so superlatively constructed by Frank Richards (or Charles Hamilton, to call him by his proper name). Greyfriars had enriched my mother's straitened girlhood in 1920s' Lurgan, Co. Armagh; and in due course it did the same for me in the Donegall Road. Most of her meagre spending money went on the weekly Companion Papers, the *Magnet,* the *Gem,* and the *Popular;* and, for a few years, the accompanying *Holiday Annuals* would appear by her bedside at Christmas. (Yes, these were among the books in our house defaced by me in my ignorant infancy – a cause of chagrin later.)

---

[16] In one book alone, Biggles and his friends, with commendable calm, survive potentially lethal encounters with a poisonous black mamba, a hungry lion, a leaping leopard, an angry rhinoceros, a coiled python, a colony of baboons; drugged coffee, a burning building, a tribe of hostile natives armed with assagais, a hair-raising take-off in a damaged aeroplane; pursuit by crocodiles; capture by savages including a colourfully dressed witch-doctor; and arrest on a (wrongful) charge of murder.

Alas, the *Magnet* and the annuals were long defunct by the time I had reached an age to enjoy them. But all was not lost, for, just after the Second World War, a bright young publisher named Charles Skilton had a brainwave. He commissioned the elderly Greyfriars author to write a series of children's books featuring the chums of the Remove and the egregious Bunter.

The series eventually extended to forty titles, of which the first ten were published by the enterprising Skilton. From 1952 and *Billy Bunter's Beanfeast*, the books came out under the Cassell imprint, but kept the distinctive yellow jackets and the Chapman illustrations. As they appeared throughout the 1950s, the Bunter books were acquired by the various Belfast libraries to which I was driven by my addiction. I had barely reached the age of reason (seven) when I first read *Billy Bunter of Greyfriars School*, borrowed from the Donegall Road branch on my mother's recommendation. I was, I suppose, just slightly too young to receive the full impact of the Greyfriars ethos, but I got enough of it to keep me attached to the series, and within a year or two I had utterly succumbed to the Richards variety of high jinks and rectitude in a blithesome public school setting.

The preeminent school was Greyfriars, indeed, but many others, each with its own excitements and enticements, flowed in a copious stream from the fertile brain of Charles Hamilton. I derived a large amount of diversion from his stories of St Jim's and Rookwood, for example, which were also appearing in book form around this time (under the pen names of Martin Clifford and Owen Conquest). But it was Greyfriars and the Famous Five, all the episodes involving wrongful expulsions, nocturnal shenanigans, detectives and crooks disguised as temporary form masters, the eventful holiday trips abroad, the incessant and exuberant goings-on: it was Greyfriars that commanded my deepest allegiance and appreciation, then and later.

There weren't enough of the books to satisfy my craving, and once again prompted by my mother and her tales of long-ago *Magnet* serials of inestimable fascination – 'The Downfall of Harry Wharton'; 'Loder for Captain'; 'Harry Wharton and Co. in India' – I wrote to the author via his publisher requesting information about the present whereabouts of the old story papers, and whether a young enthusiast might have any access to them. What did I expect? That a whole heap of *Magnets* would be parcelled up and dispatched to the Donegall Road? No: I had enough of a sense of reality to understand how unlikely it was that I would even receive a reply. However, when my letter was placed before him, the courteous old gentleman in his velvet skull-cap and dressing gown immediately sat down at his desk in Broadstairs, Kent, to answer the enquiry of a besotted small girl in Belfast, Northern Ireland, concerning the availability of old *Magnets*.

Unfortunately, his own collection had mostly gone for salvage to aid the war effort, he wrote, but he had found a copy of a pre-war *Schoolboy's Own Library* which he was enclosing. (Four of these, usually abridged versions of longer magazine serials, were issued monthly in distinctive blue and red covers between 1925 and 1940, when the wartime paper shortage put a stop to them.) You can imagine how overjoyed I was to get this gift – I still have it, inscribed to me from Frank Richards – and my pleasure was hardly marred by the fact that it featured Horace Coker of the Greyfriars Fifth Form (*Coker Comes a Cropper* was the title). The antics of fools, by and large, did not attract me; and the presence of Coker in a story brought the action as close to slapstick as it was likely to get. But the Greyfriars atmosphere – the authentic atmosphere, not the slightly eroded version of the post-war books – soon overwhelmed any reservations I might have harboured. I sent off an effusive letter of thanks to the benevolent author, who must have been constantly getting requests of this kind; and that was the end of my minuscule personal contact with the great Frank Richards.

I was fully grown up by the time an actual *Magnet* serial came my way: 'Billy Bunter in the Land of the Pyramids' it was, reissued in the original format by another intrepid publisher, Howard Baker. It featured a holiday trip to Egypt, a villain named Kalizelos, camels, kidnappings, significant scarabs and all. It was the first of many such serials, and I read them all with not the least trace of adult condescension, experiencing a degree of entertainment which would hardly have been surpassed even when I was nine or ten. The framework allowing scope for chivalry and chicanery, the handful of plots with their dexterous variations (fair play, horseplay and play for high stakes), the faintly sardonic narrative stance, the gleeful catchphrases – 'I say, you fellows'; 'All serene'; 'Bend over that chair, Bunter' – are aspects of the stories' potential for soothing and amusing. Even at an advanced age (mine), Frank Richards took me by the hand and led me up the garden path – or rather, up the Remove passage at Greyfriars School where the Famous Five under Harry Wharton's leadership are perpetually ranged against some form of glaring injustice or criminal goings-on, where Billy Bunter is continually cramming illicit 'comestibles' into his fat face, and headstrong Herbert Vernon-Smith is planning some nocturnal escapade from which his staunch friend Redwing will try to dissuade him.

'Our interest's on the dangerous edge of things', as Graham Greene has it, quoting the Browning poem 'Bishop Bloughram's Apology'; and indeed it was the bad boys with an honourable side, like Vernon-Smith – 'Smithy' – or the debonair Cardew of St Jim's, who kept my interest at fever-pitch. And thus – to quote again the irresistibly quotable Elizabeth Bowen – 'was inculcated a feeling for the dark horse'. Harry Wharton has a touch of this complexity too, and it makes him a more intriguing character than the endlessly sunny Bob Cherry (except in one serial, when Cherry uncharacteristically gets on the wrong side of everyone) or the negligible Nugent. Besides, the delinquent streak in the breakers-of-bounds and smokers-of-cigarettes has more to do with a reckless attitude, a low threshold of boredom, than an out-and-out vicious nature. For the latter, you have to turn to a character like Ponsonby of Highcliffe School who is presented without a single redeeming feature. As for Billy Bunter: his obnoxiousness is tempered by obtuseness and an absurd self-regard, and all his traits are deployed to comic effect.

And yes, I have read George Orwell's *Horizon* essay deploring the public-school world created by Frank Richards, and I applaud his astute and not ill-tempered summing up of the saga. But whereas Orwell evinces a weary exasperation with its unreality and predictability, for me the Richards set-pieces, flourishes, repetitions, contretemps, preconceptions and anachronisms all contribute to the entire oeuvre's escapist unsurpassability and against-the-odds mystique.

The great boys' story papers, in a version of the Adam-and-Eve myth, eventually engendered a female counterpart. In May 1919 the first issue of the old *School Friend* was launched. The featured school, Cliff House, originally created by Frank Richards[17] and an occasional *Magnet* tie-in, now had a weekly outlet entirely its own. The girls of Cliff House came centre stage, a position they held for some time. Not that their primacy went unchallenged. Following on from the *School Friend* came the *Schoolgirls' Own*, with a new establishment, Morcove, and a new set of ebullient Fourth

---

[17] After the first four issues of the *School Friend*, the Cliff House stories were taken over by other Amalgamated Press writers, all male.

Formers, Betty Barton and Co., to captivate girl readers during the fifteen-year period of its existence. I won't go into the fortunes of these story papers, which contributed greatly to juvenile inter-war gaiety. Their glories, ups-and-downs, and their publishing history have already been recounted with gusto by my one-time co-author, Mary Cadogan.[18] Changing fashions and wartime exigencies put paid to them. However, by 1950 the time was right for a revived *School Friend*, though in fact, when it came, the new paper bore very little resemblance to its namesake. It kept the title and something of the atmosphere, but that was all. It dispensed with Cliff House altogether, and it contained picture-strips as well as printed stories, anathema to the purist.

I preferred the stories, but I was not a purist. I was seven years old when the second or third issue of the new *School Friend* came my way, and ripe for recruitment to the followers of the Silent Three ('Careful, girls! If we're spotted we'll be for it!'), Kim the Wonder Dog, Terry Brent - Detective, and others. I was particularly taken with a picture-strip serial called 'Jill Crusoe', starring a 1900s' teenager who makes the most of being shipwrecked on a desert island. No sooner has Jill Blair stepped ashore on Paradise Isle than she rustles up a garment for herself out of big tough leaves sewn together with a fish-bone needle and strands of fibre ('My new frock is quite a success,' Jill confides to her diary). She is joined by an ally on the island, a friendly leopard called Katzi. A

---

[18] See *Mary Carries On* (2008).

native Girl Friday, to complete the trio, soon shows up in the person of M'Lani, marooned on the spot by members of her tribe due to some supposed transgression. M'Lani arrives on Paradise Isle speaking tolerable English ('If witch-doctor take M'Lani away, then surely she perish') to sidestep the language difficulty. A lot of adventures and averted South-Sea calamities ensue. At school, during the lunch hour, I spend some time contemplating the branches of trees in the wilder parts of the grounds, while considering the possibility of constructing a tree-house along 'Jill Crusoe' lines.

The arrival of the weekly *School Friend* through the letterbox caused ructions in our house, as mother, father, grandmother and myself all rushed to get our hands on it. Of course this was a bit of playacting put on for my benefit, but I didn't realise it at the time. I thought we were all agog to read the latest instalment of 'Freda's Daring Double Role' or 'Babs and Cousin Bill'.

When I moved to London in the 1960s, I left behind in the Donegall Road a tea chest crammed with old *School Friends*. At some point these were dispatched to me in West Hampstead; they accompanied us on various moves thereafter, and now reside in a wooden box beneath my desk. They survived my lapses into a blue stocking persona and elevated bibliophilia. Their preposterous contents didn't affront my newly acquired intellectual pretensions. More to the point was their remembered allure. I see myself, aged nine, glued to the exploits of their interchangeable heroines.

What you got from the *School Friend* and other papers was a session of contentment and fun. How lovely it was to encounter a plot involving expulsion or disinheritance, and see its ringleaders defeated by an unstoppable protagonist! Ranged against the good sports – who are usually Fourth Formers of high morale, but sometimes young working girls or madcap holidaymakers – are rotten prefects with names like Mabel Grudgely, odious fellow employees of the hat shop or riding stables, or ill-disposed guardians acting contrary to their quasi-parental responsibilities.

The sterling schoolgirls come out on top, but only after a lot of time spent braving ivy-covered towers (to be descended from aided by a rope), spider-infested cellars (to be locked into while mischief occurs elsewhere), spectral figures (to tear the ghostly garments off, once the initial shock is recovered from), or burning barns (to drag someone out of). The vital object at the root of all this activity, be it an elephant vase, a dragon shawl, or a black statuette, comes into the right hands in the end and establishes some wronged person's innocence. ... I'd rather not rehash any more of these threadbare scenarios. You know the story. You read it, or a version of it, when you were ten.

Alas, I am not ten and no longer relish the anodyne intricacies of the *School Friend* storylines: though, as I have said, I keep a good many specimens of the wretched ephemera by me. (All right, I'm getting into exasperated mode here; my attitude fluctuates.) When I took the stories at their face value, though, I conceived an ambition to get my hands on their colourful predecessors. Once I'd heard tell of them, I wanted to wallow in defunct Cliff House and Morcove and their pre-war frivolities. I achieved this ambition, in part, through *School Friend* and *Schoolgirls' Own* annuals of the 1920s and '30s, borrowed from friends' benevolent mothers, or discovered – joy! – on a dusty shelf of a second-hand Dublin bookshop on Ormond Quay. (The collecting instinct overtook me early.) My library at present contains complete runs of these annuals, and a good selection of the papers. Their covers sport fetching images of marcel-waved girl detectives wearing frilly frocks, unusual young form mistresses shinning vigorously down a drainpipe, holiday camp hostesses larking in the sun. I am glad to have them. But I would no more think of sitting down to read their contents than – well, than building a tree-house in the garden.

As I have already stated, this is not true of the finest *Magnet* serials, 'The Rebellion of Harry Wharton', 'The Black Sheep of Greyfriars', 'The Courtfield Cracksman', and so on: for which credit is due to Frank Richards's deep engagement with his plots and characters. You can read these at any age – well, if you're that way inclined to begin with. Unlike the girls'-paper authors (who were nearly all men, though they wrote under a variety of female pseudonyms), Frank Richards took his creations seriously. The Greyfriars stories add up to more than just an exercise in evanescence. They gladdened my girlhood, and now they help to assuage low spirits, or produce a heartening effect in times of anxiety.

Two Belfast libraries, besides those I have already referred to, were involved for a time in my obsessive reading hunts. One, of recent construction, was situated on the Ormeau Embankment and failed to embody the kind of intimate bookish ambience I enjoyed elsewhere as an adjunct to the books themselves. The Ormeau Library was too new and utilitarian to suit my peculiar tastes. I had to try it out, but I soon detached myself from it. The other library, at Ligoniel, was more in keeping with my architectural as well as with my literary requirements. It was a long way from the Donegall Road, but nevertheless easy to reach, thanks to the trolley bus route which ran from just beyond my own front gate, through the city centre, up Donegall Street to Carlisle Circus and the Crumlin Road, past Ardoyne and – about an hour after setting out – into the half-countrified robustness of Ligoniel. What you had entered then was linen mill territory: rows of stone cottages, mill buildings set in parkland, pretty Edwardian villas with flourishing gardens filled with rose bushes and steps up to their front doors, surrounding hills including the famous Wolfhill where the last wolf in Ireland was said to have been destroyed. I was sorry for this wolf, a lone survivor hunted down, and always wished it had cocked a snook at its pursuers like the Stag at Eve.

You alighted from the red city bus just opposite the

library on a hilly street, and shot across the road with your assortment of books, eager to exchange them for other vivid titles and once again disarm ennui. It was a good place to do it, small and full of atmosphere. Originally a public baths constructed in 1910 to a design by James G. Gamble, chief architect to the Belfast Corporation, the building switched its purpose from baths to books in 1946 and existed as a library between that date and 2010, when it closed its doors for the last time. Its brick-and-Portland-stone exterior made it an asset of the neighbourhood. It was chunky and charming, with its central pediment and two side wings (children's library to the right as you went in). It still stands, empty and forlorn and without a purpose. No buyer as yet has stepped in to take it in a new direction. Like the Ormeau Baths in the city centre, which functioned until recently as an interesting art gallery, its future is very uncertain.

As well as the libraries, there was in the past another great resource for the book-lovers of Belfast. It was Smithfield. Marcus Patten, in his *Central Belfast: An Historical Gazeteer* (1993), describes it thus:

> The Smithfield of popular memory was a quadrangle of small shops containing three covered arcades of junk stalls, mostly built in 1848, but the central area was built up and roofed over by the Borough Surveyor in 1884. This [was a] treasure trove of old books, old pictures, old radio components, mostly elderly dealers, and customers of all ages and classes ....

It was a place to which everyone susceptible to indigenous charm and idiosyncrasy made their way, sooner or later. It distilled the character of the wayward city. You could find anything in the cornucopia that was Smithfield from a hatpin to a penny-farthing bicycle, but what it was especially famous for was its second-hand bookstalls crammed with rare editions sitting cheek by jowl with *Men Only* and the *People's Friend Annual*.

My mother, for a birthday treat in June 1921, was taken on the train from Lurgan to Belfast by her older sister Eileen, and introduced to the ramshackle glories of Smithfield: a kindness she never forgot. On the homeward journey, in a rapture of reading anticipation, she clutched to her chest a copy of Dorothea Moore's *Rosemary the Rebel* and another book that became a firm favourite, *Anne of Green Gables* (the episode of dyeing going wrong leaving Anne Shirley with a head of green hair, had her in stitches). Move forward thirty-odd years, and in a version of the same voyage of discovery I am rooting through the corners and crannies of Smithfield, accompanied by my mother, and lighting on a cache of Gold Hawk paperbacks written by Frank Richards in his 'Martin Clifford' persona and including *Tom Merry's Secret*, *Who Ragged Railton?* and *D'Arcy in Danger*. (Another of these is the presciently titled *Trouble for Trimble*, but the humorous relevance of this to the Northern Irish situation is a long way in the future.) Oh! This is a tremendous find indeed to supplement the hardback yellow-jacketed Bunter library books. There is bred in me immediately a sense of the boundless possibilities of Smithfield, its throughother profusion.

Smithfield did not die a natural death. It was burnt alive on a dreadful night in 1974 while the Troubles raged, and terrorism, vandalism and brutality were one. The next morning, viewing the smouldering wreckage, people stood crying in the street. An indispensable endowment of the stalwart city had been destroyed: more than a landmark, more than a hunting ground for connoisseurs. 'Belfast would be nothing without a visit to Smithfield', exclaims a character in one of Bernard MacLaverty's stories; and, after the burning, Ciaran Carson takes up the threnody: 'It was great to get lost in Smithfield.' Even now, I cannot bear to approach the spot where Smithfield stood. Its absence encapsulates for me the badness of Belfast, its drive towards self-immolation.

Of course there are other, more inspiriting, aspects to the city (though nowadays I am constantly bemused by the mighty discrepancy between its past and its present incarnation. What's become of Waring Street? Where is the terminus of the Great Northern Railway? The Queen's Elms? The Ulster Club in Castle Place? Robb's Department Store? The Lombard Café? North Street Arcade? The old Ard Scoil in Divis Street? Divis Street itself, for heavens sake? I could go on. I have to go out of my way to gain the slightest whiff of an unchanging Belfast atmosphere). The libraries I knew as a child are still in place, more or less as they were (on the outside anyway). Some have gone in the direction of the Learning Resource Centre and stock their shelves (or tables) accordingly. One – the Donegall Road – has changed its function completely and become an assortment of offices. All of them contain at present only a limited selection of books-for-borrowing, as opposed to the abundance of the past. But the great Central Library at least, the Daddy of all the Belfast public libraries, has kept its reference section, its special collections and stores of antique volumes intact.

4. OLD SCHOOL FRIENDS

... the beasts loom in the green
Firred darkness of the marchen: country the child thought life
And wished for and crept to out of his own life–
Randall Jarrell, 'The Carnegie Library, Juvenile Division'

I AM EXTREMELY SUSCEPTIBLE to the power of old photographs. I have in my possession a wonderful book by Mark Kennedy called *Streets of Belfast*, which consists of images from the *Colour-Rail* archive. The speciality of this archive is transport, and all the pictures include a bus or tram in the foreground. But it's the features of the backgrounds, urban and suburban, shops and hotels, the garden walls and hedges, the houses and hills and pedestrians, which rivet my attention. It seems to be raining in a lot of these photos, which adds to the effect, and one in particular shows Royal Avenue in a downpour. You can just see the old Provincial Bank (now Tesco) at one end, with the Reform Club next to it, then the Grand Central Hotel, which always lived up to its name, followed by the General Post Office, with other buildings in the distance merging into an atmospheric blur. The pavements are gleaming with rainwater, someone, bare-headed, is running in search of shelter, and a man holding a red umbrella is visible at the extreme right-hand side. The year is 1968, when Belfast was still itself. Just beyond the barely discernible opening of North Street, and out of the photographer's range of vision, is the important Central Library.

It's a moment of transition, with the city poised to undergo a brutal transformation. Bombers, arsonists and developers are waiting in the wings to make a pig's ear of Belfast. But the library at least has stayed in place at the far end of Royal Avenue to indicate the one-time prevalence of a comelier architectural idiom. It harks back to an earlier time of change, with the old dilapidated Hercules Street in line for a face-lift. That 'Street of the Butchers', in fact, is about to be obliterated altogether, while 'A new and handsome thoroughfare called Royal Avenue'[1] comes into existence instead. And along with its other amenities, in 1884, was laid the foundation-stone of the new Free Library.

The building was designed by W.H. Lynn of the firm of Lanyon and Lynn and also attracted to itself the adjective 'handsome' as it arose in its imposing solidity before the eyes of beholders witnessing the construction of an upgraded city centre. The town of Belfast achieved 'city' status in 1888, the year the Library opened – though it took a long time before the latter settled into its supreme function, that of book-provider. It tried itself out as a museum and an art gallery at various points in its existence before its proper specialisation took over. In its

---

[1] Thomas McKnight, *Ulster As It Is* (1896).

earliest years, its News and Upper Reading Rooms drew in a lot of tramps seeking refuge from the Ulster weather and polluting the august atmosphere with their various stinks. Much later, the library suffered damage in the blitz leading to the temporary closure of its top floor. There were further setbacks and annoyances. But once it got into its stride, the Central Lending Library assumed its natural role as a book-dispensing hub from which all the little supplementary libraries radiated out.

The building of a new Free Library in Belfast was a step in the right direction. It suggested a shift in attitude from the philistinism of the nineteenth century. Before its construction, 'the only public library was in the old Linen Hall, and was rather a poor affair,' commented George A. Birmingham in his autobiography *Pleasant Places* (1934). I don't think he was being altogether fair to the venerable Linen Hall Library, and Forrest Reid would agree with me (see p. 174 below). 'George A. Birmingham' (pen name of James O. Hannay) goes on: 'But I ought not to speak ill of it, for it was a great help to me. ... There I spent many an hour reading Swinburne's works and Morris's *Earthly Paradise*'. Indeed, as a boy, he ought to have been grateful for books from the library to supplement his Sunday reading of the Bible: required reading, though, as he says, his father was sufficiently liberal-minded to recommend *Pilgrim's Progress* as an alternative Sabbath text, and never mind that 'most people would have regarded it as too exciting for the sacred day'. Under the old dispensation, culture was very much subordinate to the moral condition of the young, and Ulster fathers – well, middle-class fathers at any rate – exercised a strict control over their children's reading. The old way of thinking about books in general was focused on their potential for making young readers depraved, and this danger was greatly exaggerated in parental minds. If the book wasn't graced with a title like *Ministering Children*, or something similar, it was barred in Belfast. Not that there weren't ways round the embargo. There was hardly a boy's bed in the town, says the social commentator F. Frankfort Moore in *The Truth about Ulster* (1914), that didn't have a novel by W.H.G. Kingston or R.M. Ballantyne stuffed under its mattress; and girls were likewise adept at concealing *That Lass o' Lowrie's* or *Jane Eyre* from assiduous adult eyes.

F. Frankfort Moore speaks for spirited boys (and girls), of whom Belfast could claim as large a contingent as anywhere else. And Belfast had its own way of separating the timorous from the daredevil. *The Truth about Ulster* contains an account of the author's own overjoyed introduction to local turbulence. If he doesn't, in sober adulthood, altogether revel in the inflammable character of his birthplace, he nevertheless appears to take a kind of pride in Belfast exorbitance and incorrigibility. It all harks back to a formative experience he underwent. The year is 1857, not long after the Twelfth of July, and a careless nursemaid has conducted him and his siblings to a house in the Docks area, where she's visiting relations. Having scurried up the stairs, the young Frankfort Moore – three or four at the time – from an upper window, watches a riot in progress. Next, evading the silly nursemaid, all the little Moores run into the street and into the middle of the affray, just catching the end of the Riot Act being read by an old gentleman on a horse. The negligent nurse, running after her charges, is severely reprimanded by a policeman wearing a tall glazed hat, who instructs her in no uncertain terms to 'take them childer out o' this'. But the children have seen enough to highlight the day; and the memory of the rioting crowd stayed with F. Frankfort Moore, in all its bedlamite glory.

A childish response to the excitements of the occasion, recollected in later life, is not peculiar to Frankfort Moore, of course. The historian James Winder Good recalled arriving in Belfast as a small boy in the 1880s,[2] just as a protracted episode of civic disorder was petering out, and being riveted by the sight of policemen with rifles and revolvers massed on every corner, exhausted infantrymen dozing on the pavements, and, most stupendous of all, a detachment of Lancers escorting a mob of dishevelled prisoners, some of whom were tied to the stirrup-leathers of the troopers. 'To me,' he recalls, 'it was a blend of the London of the Gordon Riots, of which I had read in *Barnaby Rudge*, and of the Paris of *A Tale of Two Cities* – romance brought up to date.' Both the extravagant aspect of the thing, and the

---

[2] In his book *Ulster and Ireland* (1919).

sense of being – if not in the thick, at least on the edge of something momentous: these are bound to appeal to any properly alert child, and Belfast has supplied them in abundance, off and on, over the last two hundred years or so. Move forward forty-odd years from James Winder Good's sensational introduction to Belfast life, and you get John Boyd[3] lamenting his personal exclusion from the drama of street fighting: 'At home there was always talk of the riots, but, much to my dismay, rioting nearly always broke out when I was in bed, and so I had to be satisfied with the cowboy pictures I sat watching, goggle-eyed, in the New Princess. Once there was a good riot in Templemore Avenue and a Catholic spirit-grocer's shop was looted and set on fire, but when I was allowed out all I saw were the smouldering ruins.' John Hewitt, five years older (born in 1907), in his verse autobiography *Kites in Spring* (1980), records a similar scene of devastation which occurred around the same time:

> After a night when sky was lit with fire,
> we wandered down familiar Agnes Street,
> and at each side street corner we would meet
> the frequent public houses, each a pyre
> of smoking rafters, charred, the floors a mass
> of smouldering debris, sideboard, table, bed,
> smashed counters, empty bottles, shards of glass,
> the Catholic landlord and his family fled.

---

[3] John Boyd, *Out of My Class* (1980).

The point that Hewitt is making here is an integrationist one, since he viewed this sorry spectacle in the company of a Catholic friend, both of them aged fourteen or so, and beginning to move on from being exhilarated by destruction and upheaval, to deploring the sectarian imperative and all its manifestations. This is an inescapable part of growing up in Belfast, at least for those of sufficient sagacity to want to record their childhood experience, and what it signified. John Boyd, too, quickly discarded his juvenile militancy, his cowboys-and-indians ballyhoo: and he attributes his amended attitude fairly and squarely to the civilising power of literature. The public libraries, Davy McLean's bookshop in Gresham Street, second-hand stalls and his Uncle Willie's shelves all contrived to enlarge the outlook of the one-time east Belfast urchin, scholarship boy and future radio producer.

(Incidentally, there are contradictory reports about the number of bookshops in Belfast. One visitor during the nineteenth century counted fourteen, George A. Birmingham insists there was only one, and Hugh Shearman, some time later, described his birthplace as 'a very quietly self-confident literary metropolis, a city of many bookshops'. I was aware of six or so, in the 1950s.)

When did the idea first take hold that books might actually enlarge, not distort, a youthful moral sensibility? Or that books were the common property of everyone, not commodities to be made available, or not, on the say-so of bigoted church fathers (or actual fathers)? I don't know, and it's hard to say whether the Central Library was built in response to a new enlightenment in these respects, or whether it helped to foster a more liberal attitude to literature of every sort. But, during the first seventy-odd years of its existence, what is certain is that everyone in the city with an interest in reading arrived sooner or later at this crucial destination in Royal Avenue, many graduating from the smaller local libraries in emphatically demarcated districts (the Falls, the Shankill). The Central Library, like the city centre itself, was neutral territory (in sectarian terms, that is). I can't remember how old I was when I first set foot in it – ten, eleven? – but I know I possessed for years a clutch of tickets allowing me to borrow from this library along with all the others.

You entered the stately building up a short flight of steps and, once inside the great entrance hall, turned right into the children's section: a proper section in those days, stocked with everything from *Treasure Island* to *The Brydons Hunt for Trouble*. Talking of *Treasure Island* – in my opinionated youth I had something of an aversion to books coming under the 'classics' tag. (There were exceptions, of course; *Alice* was one.) I had a strong resistance to being either edified or bored, and these effects, it seemed to me, were the very thing most 'classic' authors were after, or what they inadvertently achieved. It was only when I read some of these books in later life – or reread those I had approached in a mood of defiance at nine or ten – that the point of them was revealed to me. I am thinking of works such as *The Water Babies* and *The Wind in the Willows* and *Little Women* and *The Secret Garden*, and others of equally high repute. These – or some of them – have earned their place among the exasperating classics of children's literature which affect you, the grown-up you, at some level in the way the authors intended, for all your rational dissent or ennui or critical reservations.

They may also affect you at another level. You have to applaud them in the end, but what lets you out of complete assent, in many cases, is a detectable undercurrent at odds with the surface orthodoxy. A subversive strain (which the child reader would undoubtedly have missed) has crept in and engendered a profitable tension. Charles Kingsley, for example, was a minister of the Anglican Church and a devotee of cold water, lukewarm socialism and red-hot religious feeling. And as far as the last is concerned – you have to say that very little of conventional Christianity pervades *The Water Babies*, even in the form of allegory. What you find instead is a peculiar parallel religion (as the critic Humphrey Carpenter has pointed out[4]), delineated 'with comic and sexual overtones' (which I am sure Kingsley would have repudiated). Or take *The Wind in the Willows*, which derives a lot of its strength from its embodying of a couple of irreconcilable inclinations on the part of its

[4] In *Secret Gardens* (1985).

author. Is it best to go wandering off in search of adventures, or to stay timidly, and safely, at home? Mole and the rest of Kenneth Grahame's animal characters are hard-pressed to choose between the exhilaration of striking out, and the cosiness of staying put in some familiar riverbank burrow. There are dangers, indeed, awaiting adventurers. Toad, a good fellow for all his wilfulness, has to be got out of more than one hole in the course of the story.

Nowadays I find this work more cheerful than its predecessors by Kenneth Grahame. It is inventive and unsentimental, and you'd have to concede that its impact on the juvenile reading public is not undeserved. I am happy that one of its heroes is a Rat (albeit a Water Rat), an animal that does not often come in for narrative approval. (We have to wait until 1926 and *Dr Dolittle's Zoo* by Hugh Lofting to encounter another quota of admirable rats.) ... But at any age, it seems to me, Kenneth Grahame's *The Golden Age* and *Dream Days* will overwhelm a reader with tedium and irritation. Fuss, facetiousness and the routine sneers of the day – the heroes are for ever going on about 'the female sex ... and the reasons for regarding it (speaking broadly) as dirt' – these make for dismal reading. Yet the awful books have somehow achieved a kind of 'classic' status. If I had read them at a 'proper' age, I'm convinced I'd have flung the pair of them into the fire – a reaction requiring an effort to suppress, even now. They are on my bookshelves, largely thanks to the Maxfield Parrish illustrations gracing my Bodley Head Edwardian editions, but at any moment retribution might overtake them. All right, I'm joking. I don't believe burning is a suitable fate for a book – *any* book, however reprehensible.

And as for *Little Women*, the title alone was enough to depress the spirits. Who wanted to be a little woman, when so much more fun could be got out of being an average-sized girl? And then in that book there's the terrible death of Beth to contend with (terrible in the Victorian, eyes-turned-heavenwards sense). Yes, I know it's in *Good Wives* that Beth eventually fades out of the picture, but that whole Alcott series exists in my mind as a bundle of elevated transatlantic mawkish feelings. And yet: rereading produces a slightly different assessment – one conditioned, I freely acknowledge, by the wit and insight of a marvellous essay, 'Sentimentality and Louisa M. Alcott'. It was written by Brigid Brophy and first appeared in a *Sunday Times Magazine* of 1964. With some bad temper and hundreds of reservations, Brophy says, she is forced to come out in the open 'and admit that the dreadful books are masterpieces'.

I don't know that I would go as far as that, but I have to agree that there is something appealing in the atmosphere of the opening book of the series (especially when the snow comes down and Christmas looms). As a family story, *Little Women* represents an advance on the English author Charlotte M. Yonge's *The Daisy Chain* of 1856, which set in motion the whole domestic-vicissitude genre. I've already mentioned the way in which a lot of 'classic' writing for children is fitted to accommodate some subversive strain, often to heartening effect. (This is not a new perception. I think it was Charles Kingsley who first recognised the perfect suitability of a children's book for assimilating 'an adult's most personal and private concerns', which is another way of making the same point. And: 'Most of the great works of juvenile literature are subversive in one way or another,' wrote Alison Lurie in her book of 1990, *Don't Tell the Grown-Ups*.) With *Little Women*, though, the thing that gets subverted is the progressive attitude the author started out with. You could say the novel is an account of the triumph of womanliness, as the original plan – to applaud girlhood insubordination – got twisted into something different. Alcott's heroine Jo March – who hates the name Josephine because it is 'so sentimental' – is shaped in the end by the requirements of tosh. And the book, for all its élan, ends up as the opposite of a manifesto for spirited adolescent girls with nothing to lose but their daisy chains.

If, for Louisa Alcott, the essence of childhood is located somewhat prosaically in an ultra-American, post-Civil War New England home, other writers pursuing this quality arrived at rather more resonant expressions of it. The 'secret garden' of Frances Hodgson Burnett, for example, is an image of sufficient piquancy to enliven the rather run-of-the-mill, though agreeable, story of 'character moulding' to which it is attached. (Some credit for the success of this story is due to the evocative illustrations by Charles Robinson which accompany it.) For another children's author and minister of religion, George MacDonald, a way to pin down childhood was to keep it permanent: hence, in *Lilith* (1895), his invention of a country full of children who never grew up. The only way to keep them from growing up, indeed, is to kill them off: and following on from George MacDonald, and far surpassing him in the whimsical/morbidity stakes, comes the execrable J.M. Barrie, author of a 'classic', *Peter Pan*, I really couldn't stomach, either in avid youth or more detached age.

MacDonald also wrote *Phantastes* (1858), in which the opening scene has the hero's bedroom turning into a glade in a wood. This book was read and ingested by a Belfast boy in the early twentieth century, and subsequently affected his own major literary undertaking. In the mind of C.S. Lewis, *Phantastes* joined forces with E. Nesbit's story, 'The Aunt and Amabel' to inspire the famous early episode in *The Lion, the Witch and the Wardrobe* when the back of a – what else? – wardrobe filled with fur coats opens the way into an extraterrestrial wood. Along with Lucy Pevensie, we are now in Narnia with snow coming down in buckets around us, a lamp post standing oddly in the middle of nowhere, and a debonair faun with an umbrella fast approaching.

I never reached for *The Lion, the Witch and the Wardrobe* on a shelf of the Central Library, or read its sequels as they appeared. I might have done, for the Narnia books were published through the nineteen-fifties, when I was more or less at a stage in life to get the most out of them. And there are aspects of the series I know I'd have adored: the old professor's house in the country where the Pevensie children are evacuated during the war, the striking amendment of the character of Eustace Scrubb, the militant mouse Reepicheep. But what I brought to these books when I opened the first of them was an adult sensibility, and a pretty particular one at that. I was twenty-something, and having recently cast off the shackles, as it seemed to me, of a Catholic upbringing, and graduated into the freer air of atheism, I made my way through the series with increasing disbelief and annoyance at its Christian colouring. By the time I had reached *The Last Battle*, I was taken aback to find that the 'dead children' motif, which I'd thought had vanished with *Peter Pan*, had suggested itself to C.S. Lewis in the middle of the twentieth century as a fitting resolution for the whole elaborate enterprise. (Most of the leading characters are wiped out in a train accident right at the end of the series.)

After the splendid start, with the back of the wardrobe spiralling out into a fairy-tale dimension, things (in my view) went rapidly into a decline, as Christ-the-Lion came into focus, and the whole Christian fabrication was re-enacted. This was my initial reaction, anyway, and it blinded me – perhaps – to a few of the books' incidental delights: I couldn't see the enchanted trees, as it were, for the sacred wood. And now? I'm still not completely bowled over by Narnia, but what I do admire immensely is the extraordinary ingenuity of the whole thing, with every significant incident in the seven books slotted into its place to make a perfect overall pattern.

And then there's the Ulster connection. In the Narnia series, the physical landscape of Northern Ireland keeps breaking through, as in the final pages of *The Lion, the Witch and the Wardrobe*, when the children are transported on the back of the lion Aslan, '...up windy slopes alight with gorse bushes and across the shoulders of heathery mountains ...'. In his autobiography, *Surprised by Joy* (1955), Lewis writes about his perpetual awareness of 'the stab, the pang, the inconsolable longing ... the thing itself ... the way to the world's end ... the breaking and blessing of hearts'. And we know – because he's told us, in the same book – that something akin to this feeling was first aroused in him by the sight of the Castlereagh hills from his nursery window. The four-wheeled cabs, the 'uneven squaresets' of the Belfast streets, the damp Lagan fogs, the suburban villas with shrubberies in the garden bordering flowering lawns and correctly dressed servants indoors, the nearby seaside and ships continually navigating Belfast Lough ... all these were formative influences. And if you begin in Ireland, says Elizabeth Bowen, 'Ireland remains the norm'.

The Central Library was ten years old when C.S. Lewis was born in 1898, but he has left no record of ever having visited it. Of course, in those days, books in middle-class homes like Lewis's were inherited or acquired, not borrowed. It took some time for the library habit to become widespread; and perhaps the peculiar Northern Irish combination of philistinism and puritanism contributed to the delay. (You can hear, in your mind's ear, the Revd Cooke inveighing against light literature no less than his abhorred 'theatricals'.) But by the mid-twentieth century, when book-borrowing reached its zenith, people of every class and every age were coming in droves at every available moment to change their library books.

I had got well into my stride as a borrower by this time, even if my taste in reading matter, on the whole, remained unadvanced. Library Street – the figurative location, that is, not the so-called street behind the Central – was my natural habitation. I carried away books by the armful (well, as many as I was allowed to take out using my own tickets, plus those of accommodating relatives). But what were these books, given all the blank spots I have indicated above? At ten, eleven, twelve, I was still engrossed in adventures and some school stories (not as many of the latter as I've since pursued single-mindedly as a collector). Malcolm Saville (for example) was still quite high up on my pre-teenage reading agenda; I loved the way he evoked the landscape of distinctive parts of England, distant Shropshire, the thrilling range of hills called the Stiperstones, mysterious Dartmoor, picturesque Rye, sedate, early-post-war London with its fogs and shabby Georgian squares and expensive florists' shops and chemists' windows filled with coloured jars. In the Saville stories, excitements are intertwined with places, to superb effect. 'From here they could look down over the roofs of the little town in one direction, over the river which curled round three sides of the hill in another, and, when they turned right round, they saw the rolling hills and woods which were all that now remained of Clun Forest and, in the far distance, the gaunt line of the Black Mountains, and the other tumbled hilltops over the Welsh border.' With his 'Lone Pine' series, too, I suppose I was beginning to be interested in intimations of future pairings between the characters: David and Peter (Petronella), Jon and Penny, Tom and Jenny.

Of course, any glimmer of sexual attraction in books for children was kept on an exceedingly seemly plane. It might be suggested – just – but it was never stated. The resultant evasiveness, indeed, has its ludicrous aspects. I am thinking, for example, of an obscure author I mentioned earlier, Agnes M. Miall, and how, to further one of her plots, she plants a couple of healthy adolescents, Hump (Humphrey) and Perry (a girl), in the grounds of an old manor house at midnight, and asks us to believe they have nothing, but nothing, on their minds but the foiling of a gang of smugglers. ('Their position was critical and they both knew it.') Well, why not? You encounter this situation, or something similar, over and over, in stories featuring girl-and-boy investigators of mysteries; and to push it in the direction of hormonal realities would be to disrupt the atmosphere and distort the story line. (It wasn't until the avant-garde Alan Garner published *The Owl Service* in 1967 that a way was opened for the adolescent novel to keep its compelling plot elements *and* incorporate an erotic charge.)

Actually, I'm rather glad I wasn't exposed, at twelve or thirteen, to the breezy explicitness of an all-American author like Judy Blume, who crashed through the boundaries of writing for children in the 1970s, with her upbeat treatment of perennial anxieties about delayed menstruation, untimely erections, starter bras and so forth; in one book (*Forever*, 1976) she tackles full-blown sexual encounters between two teenagers with sufficient clinical information to put an impressionable reader off the activity for life. And all in the interests of being unembarrassed about bodily imperatives and upholding socially progressive views!

Perhaps such unabashed candour and straight-faced acknowledgement of the facts of life was a necessary departure at the time, but what it heralded was a bunch of children's authors, in Britain as well as America, rushing to ground their stories in the potent realities of late-twentieth-century life. Enter the 'social problem' genre. It soon became easy for juvenile readers to find a work reflecting their real-life circumstances, especially if they were female, black, disabled, dyslexic, incontinent, homosexual, lumbered with rotten hair or fat ankles, were crammed into a high-rise block or discovered their single parent engaging in sexual hanky-panky. A proliferation of stories considered suitable for up-to-the-minute reading flooded the market. The libraries were stuffed with them. It seemed that no child's problem was too distressing or bizarre to merit encouraging treatment. You had entire novels devoted to the terminally ill. Lunacy and epilepsy were right there alongside kleptomania and teenage pregnancy. The old 'bosom friends' theme received a lesbian fillip.

And Belfast – never deemed an appropriate setting for an adventure or a fantasy or even a family story (Michael McLaverty's *Call My Brother Back* is the closest we get to one) – suddenly the dramatic possibilities of bad, cataclysmic Belfast became apparent to a host of writers. They included a number of children's authors who ran the gamut of worthiness from the creditable (Joan Lingard, Sam McBratney, Peter Carter) to the abysmal (the sort who would spend a weekend in Ballymurphy acquiring the expertise to set a story there). As a reviewer – briefly – of children's books for the *Observer* and other papers, I read a lot of these exercises in contemporary grit and social adjustment, and found the bulk of them as much in the business of edifying their readers as any Victorian death-bed-monger. Whether it comes wrapped up in sackcloth or hot-off-the-presses newsprint, a moral message is still a moral message.

Which leads me to the conclusion (again) that children's authors of the mid-twentieth century exhibit a suitable degree of reticence – and never mind if rereading sometimes produces a knowing adult smirk. We know what those adventurous adolescents would *really* have been up to, while trailing spies and uncovering secret passages and meeting for an important purpose under a laurel bush. We know, all right ... but it's not the authors' fault if readers of the twenty-first century sometimes light on an inadvertent innuendo undreamed of in the days of innocence. There's the moment, for example, when a studious schoolboy in spectacles (in Malcolm Saville's *Saucers Over the Moor*, 1955) lands a hefty punch on the chin of a crook, and afterwards exclaims in jubilation, 'That was the most wonderful bonk I've ever given anyone in my life.'

In the real world, the Central Library in Royal Avenue in the late-1950s was a place of interest for amorous adolescent loiterers-with-intent. I and a few of my would-be precocious friends were often there, on the look-out for boys, hanging around the entrance or pretending to be engaged in serious study in the august Reading Room: though what or whom we hoped to entice with our schoolbags, gym tunics and permed or tied-back hair, was a mystery. (A few years later, we might have encountered Ciaran Carson among the 'smoke-break idlers – schoolgirls, schoolboys ... on the Library steps, where lights were proffered in cupped hands, or transferred from one cigarette end to another ...'.[5]) I am sure many liaisons were formed on the spot, but we were

---

[5] *The Star Factory.*

not involved in any of them. No St Malachy's seniors, or the even more glamorous pupils of Inst or Grosvenor High School, favoured us with a second glance. To save face, we had to feign a different purpose, an obvious purpose: we were there to change our library books. For some of us, indeed, it was true – even if it wasn't the whole truth.

We were giggly provincial convent girls, not even arrived at the age of flirtation proper. There was only one beauty among us, and she still wore her dark brown hair in two babyish plaits tied with ribbons. We were just about as far removed as possible from the worldly fifth- and sixth-formers of a certain type of schoolgirl fiction (more sophisticated than Angela Brazil's). These are fictional upper-school characters of whom their authors slightly disapprove; hence their appeal for us – or at least for me. They suited my temperament, with my sneaking admiration for the 'dark horse' type. They are wayward and imperturbable. They break bounds at night to attend Hunt Balls, and set on edge the teeth of their more sporty, and sporting, fellow pupils. It isn't badness that motivates them so much as high spirits, though sometimes it requires a life-saving performance on the part of a prig to bring them to a better frame of mind. ('As if torn by an unseen hand, the planks parted just above where Mary clung, and she had an awful sensation of clinging to a rail that was falling with her to that terrible green water below. ... The rescuer was Alice, who knew that at any moment she might be plunged to a terrible death'.)

The aim is to get these classy girls to use their influence for good in the school, for they invariably have a following among impressionable juniors. They come in various guises, like the eponymous heroine of *Mary Todd's Last Term* (1939) by Frances Greenwood, who organises an entire night-life for her friends in a broom cupboard ('Girls, we have stuck together in some dreadful holes – remember the Breaking Bounds Club when we were in the Third ...'); or Springdale's Rae Murchison (in the novels by Dorita Fairlie Bruce), whose inability to refuse a dare costs her House a Banner of Merit. ('But, after all ... Rae didn't *mean* to be selfish and deceitful. She just went straight ahead for what she wanted, and forgot how it would affect other people. That's her way, you know.') Fairlie Bruce's Rae is 'naturally straight', despite her 'mad impulses', and becomes a valuable member of the upper school once guilt and dismay have worked their effect on her character.

Or take the eponymous schoolgirl in *Because of Vivian* (1947) by Phyllis Matthewman. Vivian, whose surname is given variously as Sanders and Leigh,[6] is charming and self-possessed, but somehow unsatisfactory. She doesn't discourage a sentimental attachment to herself on the part of some infatuated juniors. There is good in Vivian, though, and it comes to the fore when she bravely owns up to a misdemeanour, thereby forfeiting her prefect's

---

[6] No doubt this slip was occasioned by the current prominence of the actress Vivien Leigh, but it smacks of unforgivable carelessness.

badge. I wasn't greatly taken with Vivian when I first read this account of moral amendment, partly because she is said to be 'not very fond of animals', but also because it is true to say that neither book nor character makes a strong impression. There's a touch of 'ministering children', plus a stocky hockey brand of schoolgirl decency, about Phyllis Matthewman's stories.[7]

More to my liking is Cara St Aubrey (dubbed 'the Duchess') in Clare Mallory's *Juliet Overseas* (1949); Cara whose aristocratic nonchalance and apparent disdain for her fellow pupils conceal a doughty spirit. Cara's counterpart in the book is go-getting New Zealander Juliet Harding who has sailed in a great ocean liner all the way from Christchurch, and arrives at Queen Elinor's School in England determined to rehabilitate a washed-up House. Between the two of them – senior girls – they effect this grand purpose; though it takes some time for antipodean Juliet to appreciate Cara's English subtleties and mocking manner. The Duchess's approach to life is ironical, but you'd have to say her creator's isn't. Mallory goes all out to extol good breeding, and why this didn't, and doesn't, get up my egalitarian nose I can't explain, other than to admit there is something about the Mallory narratives[8] that compels assent. Something to do with flair

---

[7] All right, I'm not being entirely fair to this author. She created an attractive small black Aberdeen terrier called Mr Jones; and includes a couple of lively and original treasure hunts in her repertoire.

[8] She wrote ten school stories altogether.

and assurance, I suppose. And to her credit, she never resorts to life-saving, secret passages or evil form mistresses to appease the juvenile craving for melodrama.

Not that I turned up my nose at those, and worse than those, when I was ten. I remember an extraordinary trio of schoolgirl novels by an author called J. Radford Evans,[9] in which – I am about to quote a passage from Sue Sims and Hilary Clare's *Encyclopaedia of Girls' School Stories* (2000) – 'girls ... are drugged almost fatally and forced out of top floor windows at the end of a red-hot poker wielded by a maddened Fourth-former, who is subsequently beaten to a bloody pulp with a cricket bat'. This is the series in which the entire Fourth Form is rendered unconscious by a gas cannister concealed in a hamper, and in which the form captain faces a German firing squad, only to be rescued in the nick of time by a classmate disguised as a Commando. Dear me – how very unlike the daily routines of our own dear Dominican Convent on the Falls Road all this seemed.

The Falls Road and its environs have gone through a lot of incarnations. On a map of Belfast published in 1819 it barely exists; Townsend Street is literally the end of the town; and 'the Falls' is simply 'streams of water descending from the mountain, affording means for numerous bleach-greens and finishing works for linen'. I am quoting here from the reminiscences of a Thomas McTear, which

---

[9] The 'J' turns out to stand for James.

appeared towards the end of the nineteenth century. The same commentator, looking back, recalls the absence of York Street proper during the early part of that century; it was merely an opening to the rear of McCracken's cotton mill in York Lane, he says, adding that open country lay on all sides beyond Sandy Row, Durham Street, Boundary Street and Carrick Hill.

Like the name of Belfast itself, the Falls has always represented something of a puzzle for etymologists – Bóthar na bhFál, or Tuath-na-bhFál, the road of the hedges, is thought to be the most likely derivation (Fál means hedge, though it can also mean grudge or spite – perhaps we won't pursue that one); or maybe it just referred to those streams of water descending from the mountain. 'Tuath-na-bhFál', before the district got built up, was mainly a route enabling pedestrians to make their way to the top of the Black Mountain, for what purpose I do not know. To gather bluebells, furze and heather? To admire the view of Belfast Lough? To engage in sport and play? To view the encampment of sappers and miners about to start work on the Ordnance Survey? Perhaps some made the journey on foot to contemplate the scene of a sixty-year-old crime. The mountain had gained a certain notoriety back in 1753, when a householder named Richard Cole, domiciled halfway up its slope, his daughter Elizabeth and a servant called Mary Maguire, were murdered and their house burned to the ground. No explanation for this atrocity was ever proffered. It remained a mystery, so much so that it eventually led to a local catchphrase, 'It's as secret as Cole's murder.'

The excursion up the mountain was still a recreational resource in the 1950s, when the entire Falls area had gained an overwhelmingly industrial and congested overlay. Gerry Adams remembers: 'On Sundays whole families made their way up the Mountain Lonnan, past the wee tin church ... and away up the windy track to the waterfall, where the real mountain started. ... There are two paths, the lower skirting the base of the mountain and branching upwards at a number of points while the upper path reaches directly for "the hatchet field" and "the gully".'[10] I was frequently to be found on these paths myself, accompanied by my father and our mongrel collie dog, having reached the spot by cutting through the Giant's Foot Road to the Whiterock Road, and hence up to the Mountain Lonnan, or Loanen, and beyond. It was a great walk on a Sunday morning following ten o'clock Mass (boring, boring). I think of it as a winter walk though, ice formed in puddles along the lane, frozen clumps of reeds in the upland fields; and in my head, *Christmas at Nettleford* by Malcolm Saville, or the *Daily Mail Annual* with a Victorian ice-skating scene on the cover.

Seated in the Reading Room of the Belfast Central Library, and genuinely engaged in study, I might be perusing George

---

[10] *Falls Memories* (1982).

Benn's *History of Belfast*, say, his two-volume monumental work of 1880, not the skimpier version he'd brought out when he was only twenty-two, in 1823. At fifteen or sixteen, I wanted to find out as much as I could about my home town, and this seemed a good place to start, especially since Benn was intermittently very readable (whenever he brought an idiosyncratic informality to bear on his subject). I skipped the statistics relating to the water supply of Belfast in 1678, and other items of practical information; I don't think Benn was any more enthralled by these than I was, but dutifulness obliged him to put them in. He was aiming for comprehensiveness, and he achieved it, but he was also always on the look-out for intriguing snippets such as the report concerning a respectable bookseller from North Street, who, in 1816, was found lying dead drunk in Rosemary Street along with a Chaplain of the American Navy. There sprawled the inebriated pair in front of Roger Mulholland's beautiful elliptical church, no doubt causing affront to Belfast Presbyterians going about their religious affairs.

The indefatigable Benn takes us back to the beginnings of Belfast as 'a solitary castle among the desolate wastes'. The town grew slowly and was not for some time considered very desirable as a place of residence; even as late as 1690, Benn tells us, Belfast did not rank high as a healthful spot, and King William of Orange, when he came to Ireland, was urged not to linger in it on his way to the

Boyne, in case he might catch some indigenous infection. (If he *had*, I thought, the course of Irish history would likely have taken a more felicitous turn.) Picking out the bits of Benn's great undertaking that chimed with my quest for local picturesqueness – the volumes contained a section on ecclesiastical history, I remember, which I failed to read with due care and attention – I latched on to 'the fine old houses which run from Castle Place to Fountain Street', the Old White Linen Hall with its pleasant walks and shady groves (envisaging myself strolling among them in a high-waisted muslin dress and with piled-up hair), the cattle grazing in Bedford Street and women gathering 'violats' in Ye Fields[11] beyond Sandy Row in the 1680s: and contemplated these fragments of the distant past, while present drabness and insufficiency of architectural allure – a scarcity of fine old houses and the like – took a back seat.

Thinking about George Benn's 'respectable' Belfast bookseller, and brushing aside his lapse in Rosemary Street, I wonder if children's books or magazines were among the items for sale in his North Street shop, and if so, what they might have consisted of. Mother Bunch and Mother Goose, no doubt; *Little Goody Two-Shoes; Tommy Trip and his Dog Jouler;* or the very up-to-date *Adventures of a Doll* by Mary Wister, published in 1816. Or in his window you

---

[11] The great bulk of the Black Mountain would have presided over these fields, with nothing in the way of buildings between it and them.

might have spotted a local writer, Mrs Lamont, whose retelling of old stories stuck in the mind of the Thomas McTear I mention above. He singles out her version of 'Jack the Giant Killer' for special commendation. Perhaps he read it by the light of an oil lamp while seated on a wooden chair in the parlour of his aunt and uncle's house in Waring Street, where he lodged while attending a 'juvenile school' run by Mrs Lamont herself. It's 1809 or '10, and Thomas, dressed in buckskin breeches and a buff vest, is no doubt enjoying the unusually exciting story, at a time when children's reading material was rather dismally circumscribed. He was lucky, though, to be a nineteenth-century rather than an eighteenth-century reader, since contemporary beliefs concerning edifying reading had become a little more liberal, to the extent of not excluding make-believe. During the previous century, when 'rational' ideals reigned supreme, the old folk tale had fallen out of favour due to its outlandish elements. Giants and pumpkin-coaches caused Georgian parental hands to be upraised in horror. You even had Oliver Goldsmith offering to bring 'Dick Whittington' into line with the current educational policy on children's stories by cutting out the cat.

The maligned cat reasserted himself, however, with all his élan intact; and all the other fantastic beasts, with their various magical accomplishments, likewise proved impossible to suppress. Children's lives were thereby enriched. Imagine growing up missing Red Riding Hood and the wolf-

grandmother, or the Frog Prince, or the Children of Lir!
The fairy tale survived and flourished, even if it's true to say
that some of the great nineteenth-century editors of the
genre – Andrew Lang, Joseph Jacobs – were affected by the
decorum of the era, which led them to play down the stories'
aboriginal raunchiness and grit. But every generation, over
the last two or three hundred years, has had its own version
of all the thousands of retold traditional tales, adapted to
chime with contemporary niceties. They are somehow in the
very air that children breathe. I cannot remember a time
when I wasn't completely familiar with Cinderella, Tom
Thumb, Briar Rose, the Ugly Duckling, the Steadfast Tin
Soldier – but equally, I don't remember reading them. It was
as if they were simply absorbed into my system.

No bookshop in North Street existed in my day, but, for
new books (Blytons, Bunters and Christmas annuals) I had
Erskine Mayne's in Donegall Square West, and Mullan's
in Donegall Place, where the small children's section was
housed upstairs. At one time, it seems, William Mullan
& Son Ltd had a supplementary shop in Fountain Street
entirely given over to children's books; but alas, by the time
I came on the scene, this too had vanished. I know it only
from a striking photograph by Arthur Campbell, dated
precisely to 20 July 1937, which shows a group of raggedy
boys in short trousers mesmerised by the riches on display
in its window. And not a bit of wonder. If I peer very hard,
I can just make out a Biggles adventure by Captain W.E.

Johns, some titles by the publisher Ward Lock, and – I am almost sure – *Jo Returns to the Chalet School* by E.M. Brent-Dyer (the last of more interest to girls, of course).

I have to say I found no difficulty myself in ignoring the Brent-Dyer oeuvre, despite its immense popularity among a lot of my contemporaries. (*Fardingales* and *Chudleigh Hold* by the same author were exceptions, but they weren't part of her 'Chalet' saga.) Something about the atmosphere she created wasn't right for me, though – as I say – others disagreed and took her books to their bosoms. It's only as a collector that I have come to value the 'Chalet' books equally, though in a different way. Their appearance is pleasantly evocative, if not their content; and for this a lot of credit is due to the early Nina K. Brisley covers and illustrations. I'm in awe of Elinor Brent-Dyer's industry and ability to hold the whole Chalet agglomeration in her head, never losing track of the second generation pupils' family and friendship affiliations; but the Chalet stories themselves don't captivate me any more than they did when I was nine and rated them below *Molly's Masquerade at St Meg's* and other issues of the *Schoolgirls' Own Library*. This was the 1950s, but the books, having started in 1925, went on appearing year after year in a ceaseless stream. Brent-Dyer is still at it as late as 1970. Her fifty-eighth Chalet School book came out in that year, and contains the expected quota of natural and unnatural disasters. They include a thunderstorm, two floods, and a pot of green dye which falls on someone's head.

While I am on the subject of Brent-Dyer, I should mention her contemporary and fellow girls' author, Elsie Jeanette Oxenham. The books of the latter also passed me by; I don't think I had even heard her name until I began work, along with Mary Cadogan, on the study which became *You're A Brick, Angela!* At that point, I had to get down in a hurry to the business of filling some childhood reading gaps. Oxenham represented quite a large gap, for her output was prodigious. She also, I discovered, engendered total devotion among her admirers. I found her books rather good, on the whole – and better than I would have done at a more appropriate age – though, like Brigid Brophy with Louisa Alcott, I harboured many reservations. She's as easy to ridicule as Brent-Dyer and Brazil. Her girls go in for exchanges like the following:

'...Growing up is fun, you know.'
    'Is it?' Jen sounded doubtful. 'I'm not keen on it, Pixie. I want to go on playing cricket.'

They do grow up with a vengeance, however, including Jen above, and become much given to bearing twins. As with Brent-Dyer, a second generation then comes centre stage, with resultant narrative ramifications and endless intricacies. Some readers, even into middle age, keep the whole jingbang at their fingertips. The Camp Fire/Country Dance aspect of Oxenham makes a picturesque framework. Like Charles Hamilton, like Richmal Crompton, she invented an entire world complete with its own conventions, attitudes and goings-on. As a reader, you either want to inhabit it, or you don't.

Elsie Oxenham is much collected in the original editions, and this was something I could join in wholeheartedly. One by one they made their way on to my shelves: and then a great piece of collector's luck overtook me. The year is 1977, and I have come into Belfast on the bus from Strangford in County Down where I am staying with my parents during the month of August. Wandering down Donegall Pass, for a purpose I cannot now recall, I am arrested in my tracks by spotting an Oxenham title, *Schooldays at the Abbey*, complete with dust-jacket, in the window of a second-hand bookshop in a building earmarked for demolition. (I think it was Donegall Pass, but I can't be sure; it might have been Great Victoria Street. The proprietor of this shop had a habit of moving his wares from place to place: one minute it was Gresham Street, the next minute Queen's Arcade.) Nearly falling over myself to get my hands on this treasure, I enter the shop in rather a rush and stutter out my request in a flurry of trepidation. But all is well: the book hasn't vanished away after the manner of Lewis Carroll's Snark hunter. And the story doesn't end here. A couple of boxes of similar volumes are sitting out the back, I'm told, if I am interested .... In this way, an almost complete set of Oxenhams, mostly first editions, mint, in dust-jackets, comes into my possession. The total cost was under £100, but, since I was very poor at the time, I had to pay by means of a deposit and a couple of post-dated cheques. I left the place in a delirium of acquisition, utterly indifferent to the dusty pavements and sweltering city heat. The wonderful set now forms the backbone of my collection of children's books.[12]

I was especially delighted that Belfast was the source of these rare Oxenhams. It seemed felicitous that juvenile reading and adult collecting should coincide in this manner. Although, as I say, I was not in youth an Oxenham aficionado, the books themselves, with all their period lustre, make a special visual appeal to anyone interested in old-style forms of popular culture (myself among them). And to me, it adds to their interest that I know a bit about their provenance. While I stood in that blissful bookshop in Donegall Pass or wherever – whose subsequent flittings made me think of Edmund Crispin's detective novel *The Moving Toyshop* – writing out my post-dated cheques, I learnt that the Oxenham collection, bought at auction, had originally belonged to an elderly woman doctor in the city, in whose attic they were discovered after her death. It pleased me to envisage this doctor stepping out, after ministering to the ill, to make her frivolous purchases, book by book, as these were issued by the publishers, Chambers, Partridge or Frederick Warne. I see her entering the portal of the Mullans' Children's Bookshop I allude to earlier.

---

[12] I have a slightly similar story concerning the Belfast author Forrest Reid, which I will get to in Chapter Five.

What can her purpose have been? And who *was* she? I'm getting a scent of suffragette, feminist Belfast here, with its pioneering professional females and proper emphasis on girls' education, even if I'm manufacturing it out of my own nose.

Things were changing in the world at large when Mary Cadogan and I joined forces in London to write our book about girls' fiction. It was the early 1970s. A new feminist movement, under the name of Women's Liberation, was making an impact. One of its effects was to uncover, for both of us, the ways in which we had embraced a feminist ethic all along. It was partly a matter of aligning ourselves with the most active, effective and impressive characters in fiction, i.e. boys. Of course, in the books we cherished, there were girls as well to whom these adjectives could be applied, an abundance of them indeed, but sometimes their intrepidity on the page was tempered by a conservative undertone, a touch of authorial tongue-in-cheek. One of our aims was to gauge the extent to which this or that story upheld or subverted the current wisdom in relation to supposed 'feminine' limitations. We felt it our duty to come down heavily or humorously on authors who failed to meet 1970s' requirements as we perceived them.

Or at least, I did. Mary was more in the line of celebration than denigration. In certain ways we kept one another in check, and between the two of us, I think, we arrived at a tone neither bland nor upbraiding. Well, I hope we did. I was very opinionated and had it in my head that the business of bygone authors was to circumvent unpalatable beliefs, not to perpetuate them; and that our business was not to excuse offending authors ('offending' in my view) by citing the prevailing orthodoxy. I was full of the orthodoxies of my own day, which included the aforementioned neo-feminism, a kind of 'Flower Child' abandon, and a degree of sexual frankness. If you approach children's books of the past with a topical agenda, you will surely find much to discredit. I think I was very hard on authors I had long outgrown and was all too eager to repudiate. Enid Blyton is a case in point. I found myself displaying downright ingratitude for all the tremendous entertainment I had once derived from her stories (though I do believe she wrote an awful lot of nonsense, some of it verging on pernicious nonsense: *The Six Bad Boys* is an example). At the same time, I wanted to acknowledge the crucial role of childhood reading in my life (in anyone's life), and also to treat the genre as a proper subject for serious assessment (not too serious: merriment kept breaking in).

The formidable Livia Gollancz, then managing director of the firm founded by her father (and our publisher), regarded Mary very much as the senior partner in our undertaking, while I was referred to somewhat dismissively as 'that very young girl'. Looking at the photograph on our original dust-jacket, I can see what she meant; though we both look pretty young. I was old enough, however, not to be immune to an element of nostalgia in relation to my own past and every piquant factor about it: place, parents, schooldays, reading, imbroglios and all. An additional factor was the gulf that had opened between the relatively innocent past which I inhabited, and the current turmoil afflicting the North of Ireland, which I watched from afar with alarm. My birthplace seemed bent on turning itself into a slaughterhouse. The reading programme I had set myself provided a kind of refuge from this. A lot of books I had missed in childhood, and some more recent works, were central to the new critical project. I made some dazzling discoveries (of which more anon). And rereading one-time favourites, I found, brought to my mind an inspiriting echo of the setting in which I had first encountered them.

5: LOST IN A BOOK

There is, lurking at the core of every reader's engagement with the text, a double bind: the wish that what is told on the page be true, and the belief that it is not. In this tension between both, readers set up their tenuous encampment. Bruno Bettelheim long ago noted that children do not believe in the Big Bad Wolf or in Little Red-Riding Hood as such: they believe in their narrative existence, which ... can have a greater hold on us than many characters of blood and bone.
Alberto Manguel, *The Traveller, the Tower, and the Worm.*

ONE BELFAST LIBRARY WAS NOT included in my daily borrowing itinerary during the 1950s. It was the Linen Hall. The reason was simple: it was a private library with an annual subscription which placed it beyond the reach of non-affluent readers. We never aspired to enter its portal in Donegall Square North. We had the public libraries to cater to our needs, and were duly grateful for them. A fee-paying library smacked irrevocably of the middle classes, and Malone Road middle classes at that. Even a relatively well-off family like Dr Moore's (see p. 87) had no truck with the Linen Hall. As his son Brian recalled,[1] membership of that library would have struck Dr Moore as an unnecessary

---

[1] In a private conversation with P.C.

extravagance. There was also its Protestant aspect to consider. No doubt the Linen Hall had its quota of Catholic members, but for most of us lower-middle-class, under-age Catholics, it stood in its apparent aloofness for a solid, privileged, Unionist, *Protestant* side of the city. We knew nothing about its radical past, its alignment with dissent and disaffection. It was and remained utterly a closed book to us.

I first set foot in the Linen Hall Library in the company of an art school friend (yes, a Protestant) whose family's membership enabled her to select the books of her choice and carry them home. Rejoicing in the library's book aroma and dense tranquillity, I immediately got the sense of an exclusive and desirable club, and a club, moreover, whose members were not all of one kind. There was nothing to keep me from joining it myself but the limitations of a student grant. In fact, another ten years would pass before I became a fully paid-up member of the Linen Hall, a status I've adhered to ever since. It was the mid-1970s when I first paid my subscription. I lived in London at the time, and it seemed a way of reinforcing the ties that secured me to my home place. Besides, by this stage, I knew quite a bit about the library's history. The Linen Hall's past connection with radicalism and enlightenment put it in a special category. Founded in 1788 (as the Society for Promoting Knowledge), it was in the thick of Belfast politics of the day. It came out strongly on the side of the United Irish movement during the 1790s, and as a consequence lost an early librarian (Thomas

Russell, hanged at Downpatrick Gaol in 1803) and one of its original committee members (Henry Joy McCracken, hanged in Belfast's Cornmarket in 1798).

Other prominent associates of the eighteenth-century library got into hot water over the printing of unlawful material, or fell into the hands of Lord Castlereagh's militia at the library premises in Ann Street, were charged with sedition and whisked away to durance vile in Dublin. All in all, the first fifteen years of its existence were full of excitements for the Belfast Society for Promoting Knowledge. But after 1802, when the books and museum specimens were transferred from Ann Street to the middle part of the new White Linen Hall in the town centre, things settled down somewhat.

The new attitude of civic responsibility was due in part to a revulsion of feeling against armed insurrection, following the failure of the 1798 Rebellion and the Union with Britain two years later. Once the heady days of the 1790s were over, aspects of the library's democratic orientation, other than subversiveness, came to the fore. It resumed its educational function. It began to build on its association with traditional Irish music, stretching back to the Harpers' Festival of 1792 and the fieldwork undertaken by Edward Bunting. It was distinguished by its enthusiasm for antiquities, botany, local history and so forth, while anything coming under the heading of 'trivial amusement' was excluded from the library's agenda.

A lively spirit of enquiry was maintained throughout the nineteenth century, but for a long time it did not extend to an interest in current fiction, or anything of that sort. It wasn't until the 1860s that the novels of Mary Elizabeth Braddon, Mrs Henry Wood and others, began to creep on to the shelves. Even then, you feel, no distinction was made between these works and the works of authors such as George Eliot.

After having had to find a new location in 1802, the library stayed put until the end of the century, when plans to demolish the White Linen Hall and replace it with a City Hall forced another removal. This time it landed up in the building in Donegall Square North which it has occupied ever since. The Belfast author Forrest Reid, in his twenties at the time, regretted the changes overtaking the town, and in particular the loss of the graceful Old Linen Hall with its built-in library. Here, curled in a low deep window-seat, he would sit in summer admiring the view between the trees and all the way along Donegall Place, with the town's elite in their fashionable clothes promenading up and down. And no doubt, in his hands Forrest Reid held a novel by Henry James, or William Dean Howells, or Joseph Conrad, or Arthur Machen – for, as he says in his memoir *Apostate* (1926), hidden in a box below the counter, the librarian kept the latest novels for his favourite members.

The Linen Hall Library in its new setting didn't suit Forrest Reid nearly as well; he thought 'expansion had robbed it of its individuality'. It had lost something of its old and honourable position in the town. Nevertheless, it continued to draw him in, as a bibliophile, author and insatiable reader. By the time the library was well established in Donegall Square North, Forrest Reid was into his thirties and had two works of fiction to his credit. He was also getting into his stride as a collector – an omnivorous collector, for whom nothing was ruled out, as long as it met his requirements of soundness and virtuosity. Some children's books came into this category – not many, for, as he puts it in *Retrospective Adventures*, 'on the nursery shelf few treasures were to be found'. He's referring to his own childhood in the 1870s and '80s, when novels such as *Little Lord Fauntleroy* engendered in his head 'a positive loathing' (he was eleven years old when that particular account of winning ways came out in 1886); and the prolific G.A. Henty struck him as a dreary impostor. (He got on all right with Henty's friend George Manville Fenn though, whose books for boys were cast in a similar mould.)

Not much to applaud, then, apart from *Alice* (I believe no reader could possibly have anything to say against the *Alice* books – it's another matter with *Sylvie and Bruno*). And not an all-star abundance either, at the present time (Forrest Reid is writing in 1941). Some treasures, however, that came too late to beguile his childhood, beguiled to a lesser extent his middle age. They do *not* include *The Wind in the Willows*, which is castigated by him for its 'sniggering sophistication'.[2] But he's in favour of the best books of E. Nesbit, along with half of *The Water Babies* (the fairy-tale half, not the part

---

[2] I found this quality to be far more apparent in the horrible *Golden Age* and *Dream Days*.

he describes as 'a tract dedicated to the Victorian parent'). And one author in particular gains his complete approval and supplies a title for his essay on juvenile reading:[3] Hugh Lofting of 'Dr Dolittle' fame. Yes, says Forrest Reid, 'the *Dolittle* books appear to be the real thing'.

The first of these, *The Story of Dr Dolittle*, was published in England in 1922, when Forrest Reid was forty-seven years old and not, in the popular view, at a proper stage in life to immerse himself in a book written for children. But immerse himself he did, to emerge with his sensibilities exhilarated. Hugh Lofting's attitude to animals struck a chord with him – as it does with me, aside from the animal lover with all his animal friends seeing no inconsistency in eating meat. The Doctor spends a lot of time curing and communing with some and eating others. 'I smell roast beef cooking ... underdone roast beef with brown gravy over it'. All right, it's a pig speaking here; but it somehow contravenes the state of mutual esteem and amity which exists between humans and non-humans in the Dolittle universe[4] – a state which is, essentially, the point of the whole enterprise. 'Never before, I suppose, has a group of animals been gathered under one roof that had seen so much, gone to so many places and done so many things with human beings. This made it possible for them to understand the feelings of people, just as

---

[3] 'Hugh Lofting and the Nursery Shelf'.

[4] C.S. Lewis encountered this problem too, and solved it by placing the talking animals of Narnia on a par with humans, while non-talking ones remained fair game for carnivores.

knowing their language made it possible for John Dolittle ... to understand them and their troubles.'

All very fine and charming, and the 'Dr Dolittle' series is wonderfully decorative and idiosyncratic, in style and appearance. But however hard I tried – and I did try – I could not become mesmerised by the improbable voyage to Africa of a pig, a dog, a parrot, a crocodile, a duck, an owl and Dr Dolittle; or even by dramatic events in the life of a mezzo-contralto canary. I could not set aside my need for sensible or logical intrigue or a highly congenial atmosphere. The fault is mine, not Hugh Lofting's, for I read the Dolittle books (or parts of some of the books) at an even more advanced age than Forrest Reid's. And the odd thing is, what I held in my hand as I read them were Forrest Reid's own copies.

It happened in a rather roundabout way. It involves the late Northern Irish architectural historian Sir Charles (Charlie) Brett, who recommended to me the novels of Stephen Gilbert, an Ulster novelist of singular talent and small output. I read *The Landslide* (1943) and enjoyed its Donegal setting and impulse of kindness and flow of fantasy. I read *Bombardier* (1944), which vividly and dispassionately treats the author's experiences with the 3rd Ulster Searchlight Regiment during the Second World War. I borrowed Stephen Gilbert's later novels (not many) from the Linen Hall Library, and filed the lot of them away at the back of my head for a number of years.

Stephen Gilbert, said Charlie Brett, was alive and well and living in County Antrim. That snippet of information was also filed away. Then, in 1999, with my husband Jeffrey Morgan, I moved from London back to Northern Ireland – to County Antrim. Some time later, Jeff happened to spot on the motorway a van advertising an organic farm shop. He noted its address, and soon we were regular customers at the shop. It is a tremendous resource for vegetarians living in meat-orientated Antrim. Though the shop itself is not vegetarian, and does sell meat, its range of home-grown vegetables, and other foodstuffs, all denote, unusually for Northern Ireland, an enlightened way of thinking about the food we eat.

After a few weeks, the proprietor of this shop handed us a printed newssheet (we still receive a weekly news letter, but now it comes via e-mail). His name – Tom Gilbert – was printed at the bottom of the sheet, and both of us were struck, at the same instant, by a thought: is there some connection here with the elusive author of *The Landslide* and friend of our friend Charlie Brett? Well, yes, it turned out, indeed there was: 'He's my father.' Moreover, he was at that moment sitting in the kitchen across the way with his wife, drinking tea.

I didn't meet Stephen Gilbert then, but I did meet him later, briefly, when he and his wife had moved from the farm to an old people's home in a near-by town, a move occasioned by the inevitable infirmities and tribulations of age. He sat there, self-possessed though nearly blind, and failed to understand why I should be interested in his – to him – long-out-of-date works. Stephen Gilbert died in the home a couple of years later, a month before his ninety-eighth birthday. Some time before this happened, I'd been asked by his son to take a look at his father's library, which was going to have to be dispersed. Tom and his wife had plans for the farmhouse once occupied by his parents, and no space in their own house to accommodate a sizable collection of books. Eventually the problem is solved: the younger Gilberts keep some volumes, one of Tom's sisters boxes up others and takes them away, an extensive and invaluable selection finds a proper home in the Special Collections of the McClay Library at Queen's University, Belfast, and fifty or so of the remaining volumes are acquired by me.

The Stephen Gilberts' home is an eighteenth-century farmhouse with sloping floors upstairs, ramshackle and characterful in the heart of bleak, mysterious Antrim countryside. And the book-room – ah, the book-room! Let loose in here and left on my own, I'm projected backwards to my six-year-old self encountering for the first time the library cornucopia in the lower Donegall Road. But now, on top of the reader's anticipations is added the collector's instinct. Never mind the dead bat on the floor (I quickly look the other way) and the sagging shelves, here I am in my element, bedazzled and elated. And awed. In the silence and intimacy of the room, I stretch out a finger and gingerly hook from a shelf a copy of – is it? It can't be; but it is. A copy of Yeats's *The Celtic Twilight* of 1893, and laid inside it a letter from Yeats himself. I'm almost scared to look further, but of course I do; and here they all are in their antiquarian munificence: Yeats, Synge, Lady Gregory, Oscar Wilde, Padraig Colum, Somerville and Ross .... And at the centre of the collection, Forrest Reid's own copies of his own books, from *The Garden God* to *Peter Waring*, all first editions, mostly in dust-jackets – and some additional copies affectionately and humorously inscribed to Stephen Gilbert from Forrest Reid.[5]

It is well known – at any rate, in some Northern Irish literary circles, it is well known that Stephen Gilbert was a protégé of Forrest Reid's: not Reid's only protégé, indeed, but the one who followed most closely in his mentor's footsteps. I'm talking about literary practice here, the ability displayed by each to transfigure Northern Irish prosaicness and pig-headedness, in their very different ways. In *The Landslide*, beyond the black oak rafters of an old farmhouse, in impenetrable darkness where bats sleep in the daytime, lurks a ghost. For Forrest Reid, the beauty of an autumn afternoon in Belfast's Ormeau Park at dusk, with dead leaves clustered thick upon the pathways, shades into the luxuriant beauty of the Lagan Valley in summer, the grey light of winter, and then the unearthly beauty of the sea, washing for ever 'on the shores of my dream world'.

Forrest Reid's dream world, as everyone knows who knows anything about him, was awash in devotion to beauty of a different kind: that of the adolescent male. A preoccupation

---

[5] These are the books that are now in the library at Queen's, along with other Irish material from the same source.

with handsome boys has disquieting implications at present, but I think with Forrest Reid we can accept that it was all in the head (certainly no one has ever suggested otherwise). It was an aesthetic rather than an erotic preoccupation. But he made no bones about acknowledging his homosexual inclination, even if it had come upon him in a platonic form. According to Stephen Gilbert, writing in the 1977 issue of *Threshold* magazine devoted to Forrest Reid (thirty years after his death in 1947), Reid had hinted more than once that in his youth 'he had found it rather exciting to be a homosexual, as if he were a member of an elite, very secret society, a society of course to which it was slightly dangerous to belong'. He adds, crucially, 'of actual homosexual goings-on he thoroughly disapproved'.

Forrest Reid and Stephen Gilbert first met at a posh tennis club do in east Belfast. It was 1931, Reid was in his fifties, and Stephen Gilbert had just turned nineteen. They became friends. In Forrest Reid's view, the younger man was someone to be cherished and encouraged as an author and fellow dissident from every variety of Belfast philistinism. Stephen Gilbert was flattered and at first charmed by the older, distinguished author and his proffered friendship; though gradually his resistance to being 'moulded' came to the fore. Having received the full brunt of Reid's attentions over a number of years, Stephen Gilbert felt he had to take some steps to assert his own distinctive identity, which he did by becoming a wartime army recruit, by getting married, and – finally – by writing a novel in which his mentor is portrayed vividly, if not altogether affectionately.

This was *The Burnaby Experiments* of 1952 (he waited until after Forrest Reid's death before getting in his retaliation – if that's what it was – for the older author's portrayal of *him* in the novel of 1937, *Brian Westby*). *The Burnaby Experiments* is powerful and funny and strongly evocative of a bygone suburban Belfast and wilder Donegal, before an essential desolation enters in. It deals with psychic translocation, and with the attempted takeover of one personality by another, and does not arrive at a happy ending. It encompasses a darker strain of fantasy than Forrest Reid's in his 'Young Tom' trilogy (for example). And it lets us in on a few of the stresses and conflicts affecting the fraught alliance between the two Northern Irish authors.[6] Whatever their difficulties, however, their differences of personality and outlook, the friendship endured; and so, in 1947, Stephen Gilbert found himself the inheritor of Forrest Reid's remarkable library. ... Move forward sixty-odd years, and this is where I come in, with a few of the 'Dr Dolittle' books and some others under my arm.

I feel a great affinity with the book-collecting Forrest Reid, and marvel at the treasures unearthed from the small insignificant house in Ormiston Crescent, east Belfast, where he ended his days. He was in constant correspondence

---

[6] Stephen Gilbert's *Burnaby* novel outraged a few of Forrest Reid's surviving friends, including E.M. Forster who (in a letter to Knox Cunningham) called it 'disgraceful' and 'a monument of ungenerosity and ingratitude'.

with dealers, publishers[7] and fellow-authors, and must have found his living space overwhelmed by stacks of incessant acquisitions (a hazard well known to all of us unceasing accumulators). There's a word for this madness, or malady, or eccentric but worthwhile pursuit, or however you like to view it. Bibliomania. 'The disease ... manifests itself in a desire for first editions, uncut copies, illustrated copies, and "a general desire for Black Letter".' I'm quoting Ian Sansom here, in his recent book on paper,[8] and he in his turn is citing the Reverend Thomas Frognall Dibdin, who, in 1809, first brought the word into general usage with his treatise on *Bibliomania: or, Book-madness*, 'containing some account of the history, symptoms and cure of this fatal disease'.

I don't think anyone has actually died of book-collecting (well, unless they are truly mad like the protagonist of Elias Canetti's *Auto-da-Fé* and set fire to the whole caboodle and themselves along with it). It is on the other hand a life-enriching proclivity, even if it does mean for some of us going without meals in restaurants or trips abroad. The provenance of a book doesn't usually matter, as long as it's the thing you have set your sights on, but I do find it thrilling to hold in my hand some actual books once owned by Forrest Reid.

About Forrest Reid's own works I am less unambivalent. The one I find most agreeable is the charming autobiographical

---

[7] Dear Sir, went a letter of 1923 from William Heinemann, 'replying to yours of the 31st inst., The Square Book of Animals has never been reprinted ...'.

[8] *Paper: An Elegy* (2012).

Apostate, with its image of the author as a small boy in a sailor suit admiring the battered stone lions of University Square, or flattening his nose against the window of the Palm House in the Botanic Gardens. This book appeals to me more than the novels, though those too are not without engaging aspects. 'He always looked rather deeper into scenery and nature than most of us do,' said E.M. Forster, and this I can go along with. But in some sense, you would have to say, the Reid fiction is unattuned to current criteria. Something is missing, or missing for a present-day reader: vivacity, perhaps? On the other hand, there *is* that tenderness for landscape and animals and friendship, and muted romantic undercurrent .... When E.M. Forster hailed Forrest Reid as 'the most important man in Belfast', he was making an ironic observation, and obliquely criticising the bulk of Belfast's inhabitants for not being aware of the circumstance he's referring to. Important indeed. But a general indifference to literary matters should come as no surprise to anyone. That's all it was, mid-century Belfast's lack of interest in its most distinguished writer of the day; not any unpleasing impression connected with the writer himself.

I believe Forrest Reid to be innocent of any reprehensible drive (or at least, of acting on any such drive). Homosexuality is nothing now – though it meant something then – but what no one can stomach is assaults on the young. And so many horrors have come to light in recent years that you have to wonder what was going on under all our noses that we never had the smallest inkling of. Alongside a kind of perennial depravity, it seems, you had a widespread state of blissful ignorance, or naivety, a protective unknowingness. If something was unthinkable, you simply didn't think it. This is no longer true.

The thing that springs to mind is the case of William Mayne. This subtle and compelling children's author served a prison sentence in 2004 following his conviction on a charge of sexual misconduct. Children, young girls, were the designated victims here. Was he wrongly accused? I cannot say. Rumbles and rumours of something untoward had attached themselves to William Mayne as far back as 1973. Then, more than thirty years later, came the accusation by a Yorkshire farmer's wife in her fifties of abuse at the hands of the author, starting when she was eight and continuing over a period of six years. (I have to ask myself – why didn't she speak out sooner? Or, at the time, keep well away from the person inflicting the damage? But what do I know? Such goings-on are utterly outside my experience, and outside the experience of others I'm acquainted with.) And for some, I suppose, the Mayne oeuvre has become all the more bothering because of its innocence of feeling.

He saw how the sunlight fell behind the trees opposite, and shone down on to more clearings: they showed yellow behind the dark trees that fringed them and the Mere. And over there was the absolute peace of a quite unknown land where no man had walked or travelled. And the proper way to get there, he knew now, was not by land, but by water: there was old England waiting to be discovered and dwelt in; and this side of the Mere was no magic place but the old and tired land of the present inhabitants.

This passage comes from *The Blue Boat* of 1957, and so does the following:

> There was a wood outside, and there were squirrels leaping in the trees, and in the clear spaces below the trees half a dozen great black birds walking; and under the window two budgerigars standing on a stick, and at the other end of the wood was a stumpy square animal, brown and black, digging slowly and looking for something. It was a bear.

I find it painful to think of the author William Mayne convicted of a shocking and unsavoury crime and forced to undergo a petrifying prison sentence. I also find it painful to think of people trawling through his bewitching stories on the look-out for salacious implications. There were those who called for his 'tainted books' to be banned altogether: though even without that blanket embargo, Mayne novels tended to be quietly removed from libraries and bookshops, leaving the field of children's literature woefully impoverished. This was an author of a rare delicacy of touch, with a mastery of the mysterious and profound. He's both lyrical and robust: his books are saturated in the particulars of an inspirational locale, the Yorkshire Dales.

The first Mayne title, *Follow the Footprints*, was published in 1953 and no doubt sat before my eyes on a shelf of one or other of the Belfast libraries which I frequented. But whatever I lifted from the same shelf, it wasn't that. I was too caught up with Enid Blyton (or her near namesake, Enid Boyton[9]) to want to try out anything so conspicuously different. Not that *Footprints*, the story of a fairly routine treasure hunt, is as striking or enigmatic as the later Mayne fiction became. Once this author had arrived at his own distinctive method, it seemed that nothing in the way of innovation or evocation was beyond him.

He was part of a sudden resurgence of excellence in children's literature which began in the 1950s and continued for the next twenty-five years or so.[10] I'm thinking here of what you might call the Garner-Garfield-Gardam efflorescence. These were the writers I fell on with whoops of delight when research for *You're A Brick, Angela!* obliged me to retrieve my old susceptibility to the world of make-believe (or perhaps I had never lost it).

Some of their books I had on loan from the small children's section of the Linen Hall Library. Though I was based in London at the time (the mid-1970s), I was often to be found back home in Belfast, staying with my parents in the Donegall Road. (This was before they moved to the County Down coast.) So I was back where I started, devouring

---

[9] Pseudonym of Horace E. Boyton, an occasional contributor to the 'Schoolgirls' Own Library' series.

[10] It was followed, as I mention above (P. 148) by an equally sudden decline into a 'social problem' genre; what happened after that I'm not equipped to say, except that - along with everyone else - I greatly admire J.K. Rowling and Philip Pullman.

fiction in my tiny childhood bedroom still with its pale
blue wallpaper and quilted satin eiderdown. I read on and
on, into the small hours, while Belfast erupted in violence
around me and flames from a burning bus illumined the
pitch-dark sky. The stricken bus burned down to a tangle of
smouldering metal, hardly a stone's throw from where I sat
propped up on pillows, far from the perils of the night – in
spirit at least. I was falling back on a childhood resource.
But now it was Jane Gardam who kept me awake rather
than *Jane Gets Busy*, *The Children of Green Knowe*, not *The
Children of Kidillen*. [11]

   Green Knowe. Could anything be more delectable,
or further in spirit from the saddening and sickening
Ulster tumults, than Lucy Boston's magical house and the
stories it engendered? The house is real, a twelfth-century
Cambridgeshire manor house, the author's home for more
than half a century, and its imagined inhabitants are a triumph
of sensitivity and creativity. It grows into a candle-lit, stone-
staircase, cherry-blossom kind of enterprise. In Book One of
the series, *The Children of Green Knowe* (1954), a small boy,
Tolly, comes to live with his great-grandmother in a house
whose name is either Green Knowe or Green Noah. Here
is the first ambiguity. And here is another: there are children
about the place, mischievous, playful, enigmatic children,
with names and pets and personalities, even though they died

---

[11] All right, the phrase 'fiddling while Rome burns' is not excluded from my
consciousness.

in the Great Plague of 1665. We're face-to-face with a 'Burnt Norton' turn of events: 'Even while the dust moves/There rises the hidden laughter/Of children in the foliage.' 'Ghosts' is too uncouth a title for suchlike presences.

'I like this house,' says Tolly in the first sequel, *The Chimneys of Green Knowe*. 'It's like living in a book that keeps coming true.' If things that shouldn't, keep coming alive, it's just a way of adding mystery and enrichment to the commonplace. As with William Mayne's, these radiant works of fiction might have gravitated towards me at a suitable age: my loss that they didn't. Gillian Avery too: I'd just about have been able to be beguiled by *The Warden's Niece* when it was published in 1957 (though by then I had graduated to Agatha Christie and P.G. Wodehouse). The warden's niece is Maria, who, in the opening pages, runs away from a stupid school for young ladies and makes her way to Oxford and her great-uncle Hadden, Warden of the fictitious Canterbury College. The year is 1875, and Maria, aged eleven or thereabouts, has an ambition to become a Professor of Greek in later life. In the meantime she undergoes a series of embarrassments, partly occasioned by an elongated tutor she shares with three boys next door, a Mr Copplestone. 'Oh, Copplestone ... there's no knowing what he'll do.' For Maria, having to crawl on her hands and knees out of the Bodleian Library, past the alarming librarian, is only the start of it. She does, however, despite enormous obstacles, succeed in carrying out a piece of original research, and (off-stage) reads a learned paper on it before the Kentish

Historical Association. Thus is a small blow struck for women's emancipation, playfully and posthumously.

At nineteen, as an art student in Belfast and an Irish-language enthusiast, I would really have been too old and snooty to pay attention to Joan Aiken's *The Wolves of Willoughby Chase* when it first appeared in 1962. (Though I might have relished it surreptitiously, had it come my way.) Twelve years later, sanctioned, like Maria Henneker-Hadden, by the term 'original research', I was free to succumb to its fairy-tale, harm's-way shenanigans. ... A couple of brave girls, Bonnie and her orphaned cousin Sylvia, consigned to an awful orphanage by their governess Miss Slighcarp, run away in the middle of the night, aided and abetted by a denizen of the woods, a ragged boy named Simon. Simon, of course, as it turns out, is of royal birth. Joan Aiken takes the conventions in hand and imposes her own blithe stamp on them. If it's blatant appropriation, it is also new-style wit and homage.

The 'Willoughby Chase' series, which eventually runs to eleven titles,[12] next shifts the scene of action to London, where the boy Simon comes centre stage. But – although he features prominently in subsequent stories – Simon is soon displaced from his central position by a stout-hearted, resourceful Cockney tatterdemalion named Dido Twite. The book in which it happens is *Black Hearts in Battersea* (1965) – and by this stage in the saga it is plain that nineteenth-century England is not the place with which historians are

---

[12] The last, *The Witch of Clatteringshaws*, was published posthumously in 2010.

familiar. Joan Aiken triumphantly wrenches the English succession off-course. The Jacobite line is in the ascendant, and Hanoverian plotters lurk in every corner. In a time that never happened, *anything* can happen – and it does. We are bombarded with exuberant and exorbitant goings-on. A proposed assassination of King James III by long-range gun from America isn't the half of it.

Around this time I also encountered, with jubilation, the aforementioned Garfield-Garner-Gardam phenomenon. Each of these luminaries of children's writing in the 1960s and '70s extended the scope of the genre and ensured that it would never be the same again. Respectively endowed with a Dickensian aplomb, with an electrifying way of presenting up-dated West-Country lore, and with an arresting line in mid-century adolescence, they make a fabulous trio. Add Penelope Lively with her subtle excavations and patterns of continuity, and Philippa Pearce, who, in *Tom's Midnight Garden* (1958), engagingly tampers with linear time, and you might get an inkling of the way the whole field of children's writing had suddenly arrived at an unprecedented virtuosity. (I shouldn't forget authors such as Jill Paton Walsh, Penelope Farmer, Nina Beachcroft, Geraldine Symons and others, but I don't want to rehash the final chapters of *You're a Brick, Angela!*, or stray too far from my current theme.)

At a certain point, it seems, children's literature grew up, and it's been growing up in different ways ever since, with old themes and preoccupations falling into ever more dense and ambitious configurations. You cannot get away from the fundamental storyline featuring a child, or group of children, going all out to reverse some monstrous injustice, or avert a looming calamity – only now it's more likely to be a threat to the universe than a plot to unseat the form captain. All the themes and devices are attuned to current requirements. For example, the threadbare girl detective, Nancy Drew, has given way to the infinitely more cogent and entertaining boy lawyer: Theodore Boone, in John Grisham's recent series aimed at the Young Adult market. (These books are aligned to a twenty-first-century departure: the unexpected incursion of adult thriller writers such as Kathy Reichs, Elizabeth George, Harlan Coben and others, into the teenage fiction genre.)

Well, I thought, back in the mid-1970s with my nose in *Green Knowe*, this is a great way to earn a living, albeit a very moderate living. It certainly beats being an unreconciled art mistress in a Battersea grammar school, or proof-reading bits of balderdash for Mills & Boon (both constituents of a post-art-school, floundering professional life). And having got the children's-books-bit between my teeth, so to speak, I've never let go of it – though for me, the juvenile genre is of course subordinate to other kinds of reading. In Belfast, in County Down, in London, and now in Antrim where I've lived for fourteen years, an occasional piece of fiction intended for a teenage or younger readership has found its way into an inappropriate pair of hands, i.e. mine. Well, narrative is narrative, whatever age it's aimed at, and stories fix our way of seeing the world, no less at sixty than sixteen, or six. It's essentially a matter of accretion. *My* Belfast is an amalgam of what I have actually experienced through growing up in the city, and what I've experienced vicariously through reading about it, in every form of literature. And not only that. The books I've read, the vast majority of them, have nothing whatever to do with Belfast, that speck in the universe, but they have – inevitably – coloured my attitude to its goings-on, its sects and shambles, its history and hysteria and pockets of pure delight.

Among the pleasures consequent on returning to one's birthplace after a long absence is the possibility of renewing lapsed friendships. More often than not, an element of happenstance comes into it. You bump into someone in the street, in a café, on the way from the dentist, who tells you, so-and-so will be in such-and-such a place later. You sit down to wait. You enter a charity shop and find an old classmate behind the counter. Someone taps you on the shoulder at a social gathering saying, Is it? It can't be .... You don't quite believe it either. But it is. Never seen or heard of for half a lifetime. And sometimes, though rarely, you can take up where you left off, all that time ago. More often, of course, this doesn't happen; each of you has diverged too radically from the preoccupations that drew you together at nine or ten; life has turned you into persons no longer congenial to one another. You smile, agree to keep in touch, all the while knowing you won't. But how charming, how reassuring, when the thing immediately clicks into place, just as it did in the first instance.

At the present time, a trio of former school friends, happily reunited – Fiona (Devlin) Coyle, Mary (Stinson) Cosgrove, and myself – get together every six weeks or so to drink tea or coffee and rehearse old contretemps in the café attached to the Linen Hall Library. It's an appropriate meeting place for a number of reasons, though I have to say I deplore the transformation of the august old Linen Hall reading room into a version of P.G. Wodehouse's 'godforsaken eatery'. We, the three of us, enjoy stepping back in time, as well as engaging in present-day gossip and literary dissection. And the setting, once you get over the food aromas and café clutter, imposes a kind of cultural and personal continuity on the course of our entirely dissimilar existences. Whatever else befell us, we were all, always, library aficionados.

I needn't go into our varied histories here, but it might be in order to revisit, for a moment, the distant past and the points of departure from which has resulted our present Triple Alliance. (I'm quoting the boys' author Harold Avery here.) So here goes: I am four years old, a midget pupil in the Kindergarten Department of St Dominic's School on the Falls Road, when into our infant-orientated classroom – chalk, crayons, coloured paper, plasticine, milk bottles, holy pictures, minute desks and an enormous nun wearing an apron on top of her cream serge habit – into our classroom walks a sturdy child with reddish brown hair screwed into unnatural ringlets and an expression half-scornful, half-apprehensive on her face. She is accompanied by a figure I know as the head nun, who tells us, Now, children, here is a new little girl. Her name is Fiona,[13] and I want you all to be very kind to her – at which point the new little girl called Fiona glares around the room and all but bares her teeth. The thought crosses my mind: here is a possible kindred spirit, an antidote to all the prigs and ninnies, the 'Oh Sister, please Sister' brigade by whom I am surrounded. And so it proves. Soon we are sitting together at adjacent desks; we enact the childhood rituals of the Catholic Church side-by-side; we accompany one another to our next school, Aquinas Hall, and back again – post-Eleven-Plus – to the Falls Road Dominican Convent which has long dispensed with its Kindergarten and is now exclusively a grammar school.[14]

On it converge, around nine in the morning, hordes of maroon-clad girls with schoolbags strapped to their backs, some carrying hockey or camogie sticks, some – rebels – bare-headed, but most wearing the regulation school beret with its black-and-white crest. All of them streaming towards the school's several entrances like sacrifices to some kind of indigenous Moloch. 'Girls!' (I'm appropriating a similar scene described by Angela Brazil) 'Girls everywhere ... tall

---

[13] Spelt like that, but pronounced 'Fianna', as in 'Fianna Fáil'.

[14] My ignominious departure from this school is the subject of my memoir, *Asking for Trouble* (2007).

girls, short girls, fat girls, slim girls ... everywhere, girls!' You could be overwhelmed by girls if you let yourself – or so it seems to me and my friend Fiona, very new pupils about to take our place in the basement classroom presided over by a Sister Consuelo, and try to get the hang of the school ethos.

Among our new classmates is an attractive, fair-haired, out-going girl called Mary. In my view – looking back – Mary, Fiona and a handful of others detach themselves to some degree from the stolid Dominican schoolgirl rank-and-file. To begin with, they possess qualities which chime with my bookish outlook on things. They are clever,[15] amusing and slightly at odds with the more repressive side of the school spirit. They are readers of light literature (*School Friend, Girl's Crystal*) as well as teachers' choices (Jane Austen, Robert Louis Stevenson), and of enthralling adventure stories picked by themselves from the shelves of any one of Belfast's Carnegie libraries. The Falls Road branch, being closest to St Dominic's, is the one they – and I – tend to make a beeline for, at the end of the school day. Here – among other delights – we pounce on stories geared to instruct us in behaviour appropriate to our position in the school. "'Hello, you deplorable infants, said Lalage Stephens, ... "What an atrocious noise you are making!'" They alert us to the constant need for self-suppression – "'I hope Miss Lucas is not hurt," said Miss Gray coldly; while

---

[15] In our end-of-term tests, the two I've named quite often achieved the top position in the class, whereas I never did.

the girls tried not to laugh at the idea of one of the mistresses falling into the cucumber frame' – and underscore the importance of unspoken rules: ' "Inside the school grounds you can run until - until your knees sag, but outside you have to remember to be A Credit to the School." '

Thinking about being A Credit to the School brings me to a conference I attended at Edinburgh University a few years back. The subject was Children's Literature, and the thing that struck me was the really amazing way the delegates, to a woman, fell into roles familiar to all of us from our childhood reading. First comes the handsome Head Girl whose glance is sufficient to quell any sign of insubordination. 'By the force of her convictions and example she had inspired the school to reach incredible heights of hard work and enthusiasm.' The Head Girl has her acolytes, 'loyal, useful members of their form', who see to it that her instructions are carried out. ' "Do as you're told, Shirley, and don't argue." ' She, the top dog, is gazed at with awe by an impressionable New Girl (this one an American follower of the genre, years younger than most of us middle-aged delegates), who comes close to making a nuisance of herself. 'Phyllis thought Lois a silly little thing, and she wished she would leave her alone.' Prefects put in an appearance, including the Games Captain whose watchword is Fair Play, and the Efficient Organiser who arranges the seating at evening meals. Then we have the Artistic Talented Sixth-Former – 'She was a pretty, fluffy-haired person, small, graceful, and the most competent artist Dewhurst had ever produced' – in this case, an attractive children's author and guest of honour, who appears at dinner wearing an elegant dark green velvet dress. Next, enter the Bossy Boots, who specialises in throwing her weight about. 'She was blunt to the point of rudeness, sporting, certainly, but utterly devoid of either sympathy or imagination. ... "Don't be an idiot," she said. "Those juniors can't be allowed to give impudence all round without suffering for it."'

Even lower in the scale of popularity comes the Horrid Sneak (no Fourth Form complete without one) whose unattractive personality contains elements of moping and moaning ('Irma gave a scowl'). The present Sneak succeeds in annoying or offending everyone who attempts to make conversation with her, and her behaviour gives rise to colloquies in corners criticising it. One of her gripes concerns the failure of the School to accord her the attention she craves; as a consequence, nothing is right for her. ('A moment later Eva Mappin entered, her unpleasant face set in a slight sneer.') She does her best to sow discord. But aside from this blip, good spirits prevail. And these are due in part to the presence at the Edinburgh gathering of a debonair, scholarly and flamboyant figure: a Famous Uncle returned from a lengthy fossil-hunting voyage, as it may be; or Dr Dolittle himself with all his inventiveness and amiability. Not that 'Dolittle' fits the bill. (It didn't for him either.) At this point I am going to come out in the open and identify this person as Owen Dudley Edwards, Dublin-born, Edinburgh-domiciled, and the author of – among other things – a monumental and diverting work entitled *British Children's Fiction in the Second World War*. This wonderful book applauds unassuming juvenile fiction as an incomparable resource in wartime (or indeed, at any time), giving due credit to popular authors such as Blyton, Brent-Dyer, W.E. Johns, Richmal Crompton *et al*, whose achievements are substantially and sympathetically appraised.

Among the schoolgirl characters enumerated above I nearly forgot one – perhaps not surprisingly: '"She's a nonentity, but she's got quite a nice way with her."' This is the Good Sport, last seen in Edinburgh gamely plodding in the wake of The Lower School Leader, while the latter merrily conducts a party of appreciative Third Formers around and about the Royal Mile. ... Step off this main thoroughfare and you're bang in the middle of dark alleyways between tall houses, old stone-paved courtyards, back garrets, overhanging gables and hidden gardens, narrow entries ending in 'twisty, corkscrew staircases', streams of washing flapping in the wind. (All right, there wasn't any washing; I'm paraphrasing one of Elisabeth Kyle's evocations of Edinburgh in her charming children's novel of 1954, *The House of the Pelican*. Did I once have it on loan from the Donegall Road library? Yes.)

Actually, there's another Edinburgh delegate to whom I nearly forgot to allocate a suitable role: myself. It seems I have placed myself, by default, among those anonymous sight-seeing Third Formers revelling in the light and shade of the wynds and closes, 'the curious old corners', the picturesque disarray. Quite fitting. But now I recall a title by Phyllis Matthewman, whom I mentioned earlier (p. 152), that might furnish a clue to my view of the Children's Books conference, or its of me. *The Intrusion of Nicola.* The eponymous Nicola is not a normal schoolgirl, and I, I think, am not a normal conference-goer.

It is partly the lack of a university background. Without a Miss Jean Brodie to equip me for the *crème de la crème*, I've had to enter the field of literature, or literary criticism, sideways, as it were. I don't regret this, but it does give me a slightly different perspective on things academic or institutional. I am detached from their routines. Certainly I never aspired to be Sandy Stranger – well, I wouldn't, would I? She became a nun – but the novel in which she appears is one I carry with me, in my head, and has been since I first read it shortly after its publication in 1961. And of course I can't set foot in the Royal Mile without recalling the scene in which Miss Brodie leads her charges on a bracing History Walk –' "John Knox,' said Miss Brodie, 'was an embittered man ..."' – and incidentally introduces the well-bred, 1930s' girls of Marcia Blane School to the disquiets of the slums. 'Children and women with shawls came in and out of the dark closes.'

As Millfield/Peter's Hill was to Belmont or the Malone Road, so the dark closes were to the Morningside area of

Edinburgh where Muriel Spark – Muriel Camberg as she was then – grew up in the 1920s and '30s and devoted herself to literature (poetry in particular). 'At least twice a week after school, I would go the public lending library in Morningside. ... I would bring home four books at a time, most of them poetry .... Nineteenth- and twentieth-century poets were my preference.'[16] She had started early along these lines with *A Child's Garden of Verses* – especially to be appreciated by an Edinburgh child – and gained from it an understanding of the difference between the old-time lamp-lighter and the more recent one who carried a pole to turn on the gas-light, rather than a cumbersome stepladder. (Leerie posting up the street had got into my imagination too, even though our street-lamps came on automatically in St James's Avenue and the Donegall Road.) Later, Spark says, she felt an affinity with the Robert Louis Stevenson of the *Picturesque Notes*, his insightful Edinburgh evocations. 'You go under dark arches [he wrote], and down dark stairs and alleys. The way is so narrow that you can lay a hand on either wall ... the houses bulge outwards upon flimsy brackets; you see a bit of sculpture in a dark corner; at the top of all, a gable and a few crowsteps are printed on the sky.'[17]

Though I don't know them well, those dark Edinburgh arches and alleys suggest to me the ultimate in historical and architectural richness, romantic, sinister and Jessie M. King

---

[16] Muriel Spark, *Curriculum Vitae* (1992).

[17] Robert Louis Stevenson, *Picturesque Notes* (1879).

decorative. (All right, I'm blocking out their slum aspects.[18]) They teem with associations. We had nothing comparable in Belfast, and what we did have – the narrow lanes between Ann Street and High Street, say – has been utterly divested of any vestige of character. Crass planning decisions have made short work of the historic town. I think again of the long-obliterated, never-seen 'fine old houses' running from Castle Place to Fountain Street. Alas.

But I shouldn't be too down-hearted: Fountain Street at the present time contains the back entrance to the Linen Hall Library, that treasure house of information and entertainment, and when I consider how close the library came to extinction in the shattering 'Troubles' era, I bless the impulse that kept it going, outwitting the fate that had seemed foredestined. With everything collapsing around it, it nearly collapsed itself. The recently retired librarian John Killen, in his *History of the Linen Hall Library, 1788-1988*, calls his penultimate chapter, 'Decline'; but decline, Alleluia, was not the end of the story. It was followed by 'Resurgence', as strategies were put in place to ensure the library's survival. Even during the dark days of nearly incessant city-centre savagery, though, there were those who braved the bombers and arsonists, the disruption and horror and menace, to gain for a moment a sense of a different Belfast, a place of enlightenment not backlash, an urbane approach to life instead of dog-eat-dog. As Seamus

[18] Another view of these dark places is to be found in the work of the great Scots Gaelic poet Sorley MacLean.

Heaney put it, 'the moral and imaginative quickening that took place in the late eighteenth century always revives for me when I go up [the Linen Hall] stairs'.

Continuity, accretion and connection. Throughout this book, I have tried to place these in a Northern Irish context, specifically in relation to literature (in the broadest sense), mainly children's literature; and to suggest the ways in which the reading habit, once acquired, can work against the things it is right to deplore, the bigotries and antagonisms that come at us in the North from the word go, and sometimes find a lodging, like the splinter of glass in the heart of Hans Andersen's Kay. Reading takes the harm out of life's shocks and setbacks – or at least dilutes these, or puts them in perspective. It provides links across time, across countries and continents. I'm thinking, for instance, of Clive James in Kogarah, Australia, with his beloved Biggles books laid out before him on his childhood bed; and just a few years later, Ciaran Carson in Andersonstown, Belfast, with *his* Biggles books supplying balm and consolation. Or, if I take myself and my Frank Richards addiction, I can tie it in with my mother's absorption in the same author's stories in Lurgan, Co. Armagh, in the 1920s, and with my co-author Mary Cadogan's equal enthusiasm for Greyfriars in 1930s' and '40s' Beckenham, Kent. Sludge, Clive James calls this type of reading when he looks at it in sober middle age – with Biggles memorably classed as 'flying sludge'. But, he goes on, post-Biggles, 'I continued to read everything that was real, and I still do. [And] I got the habit by reading everything that was false.'[19]

False, I would add, only in the tongue-in-cheek, not the inimical sense, and 'true' or 'real' to different degrees: that is, to be accepted utterly, or partially, for the duration of the story, in the realm of the imagination. And it – the remembered atmosphere of a piece of fiction – never wholly evaporates. Lost time, time passing and retrievable time are all there at the turn of a page. The fusion of realism ('We're going to Kew to see the magnolias') and make-believe ('It was on a Saturday that the children made their first glorious journey on the wishing carpet') works wonders. For all of us tenacious readers, there are more worlds to be inhabited than the real one, more excitements to be undergone, initiatives to be applauded, doors to be opened, thresholds to be crossed, resolutions to be savoured, nettles to be grasped, mettle to be cheered, rose-gardens to be visited, myths to be assimilated, children among the leaves to be glimpsed, mysteries to be illumined, lights to be seen, prairies to be explored, revelations to be encountered, evocations to be submerged in, pasts to be resurrected ... and more, and more. Here's Louis MacNeice in responsive mode, revisiting his home town of Carrickfergus: 'And the child's astonishment not yet cured.'

---

[19] Clive James, 'Starting with Sludge'. *Times Literary Supplement*, 16 December 2005.

SUGGESTED FURTHER READING

Mary Cadogan, *Mary Carries On*. Girls Gone By Publishers 2008

Mary Cadogan and Patricia Craig, *You're a Brick, Angela!* Victor Gollancz 1976; new edition Girls Gone By Publishers 2003.

Humphrey Carpenter, *Secret Gardens*. George Allen & Unwin 1985

Ciaran Carson, *The Star Factory*. Granta Books 1997.

Owen Dudley Edwards, *British Children's Fiction in the Second World War*. Edinburgh University Press 2007.

Susan Hill, *Howards End is on the Landing*. Profile Books 2009.

Alison Lurie, *Don't Tell the Grown-Ups*. Bloomsbury 1990.

Alberto Manguel, *A Reader on Reading*. Yale University Press 2010.

Ian Sansom, *Paper: An Elegy*. Fourth Estate 2012.

Patricia Mayer Spacks, *On Rereading*. Belknap Press 2011.

Francis Spufford, *The Child that Books Built*. Faber & Faber 2002.

ACKNOWLEDGEMENTS

I should like to thank the Arts Council of Northern Ireland, and especially Damian Smyth, for much appreciated help and enthusiasm during the writing of *Bookworm*. The Society of Authors, a tremendous resource for writers, also helped financially and by supporting the project. I'm deeply indebted, too, to my astute and indefatigable agent Jonathan Williams, and to Andrew and Jane Russell of the splendid Somerville Press. Thanks too to their brilliant designer Jane Stark. I'm grateful to those friends with whom I've discussed the subject of this book, including fellow-childhood-readers Fiona Coyle and Mary Cosgrove (to whom *Bookworm* is dedicated), Polly Devlin, Anne Devlin, Patricia Mallon, Val Warner and the late Naomi May. An inestimable debt of gratitude is due to my late mother Nora Craig, who made me an unstoppable reader; and to my husband Jeffrey Morgan, for constant encouragement and intellectual stimulation. My one-time co-author Mary Cadogan died before I was able to send her a draft version of *Bookworm*; her comments would have been valued. The book is also dedicated to her memory.